Pairs
Trading

Founded in 1807, John Wiley & Sons is the oldest independent publishing company in the United States. With offices in North America, Europe, Australia, and Asia, Wiley is globally committed to developing and marketing print and electronic products and services for our customers' professional and personal knowledge and understanding.

The Wiley Finance series contains books written specifically for finance and investment professionals as well as sophisticated individual investors and their financial advisors. Book topics range from portfolio management to e-commerce, risk management, financial engineering, valuation, and financial instrument analysis, as well as much more.

For a list of available titles, visit our Web site at www.WileyFinance.com.

Pairs Trading

Quantitative Methods and Analysis

GANAPATHY VIDYAMURTHY

WILEY

John Wiley & Sons, Inc.

For general information on our other products and services, or technical support, please contact our Customer Care Department within the United States at 800-762-2974, outside the United States at 317-572-3993 or fax 317-572-4002.

Wiley also publishes its books in a variety of electronic formats. Some content that appears in print may not be available in electronic books.

For more information about Wiley products, visit our web site at www.wiley.com.

Library of Congress Cataloging-in-Publication Data:

Vidyamurthy, Ganapathy.
    Pairs trading : quantitative methods and analysis / Ganapathy Vidyamurthy.
      p.   cm.
    Includes bibliographical references and index.
    ISBN 0-471-46067-2 (cloth)
    1. Pairs trading. 2. Stocks. 3. Portfolio management. 4. Investment analysis. I. Title.
HG4661.V53 2004
332.64′524—dc22

                                       2004005528

Printed in the United States of America

10 9 8 7 6 5 4 3 2 1

Contents

Preface

Most book readers are likely to concur with the idea that the least read portion of any book is the preface. With that in mind, and the fact that the reader has indeed taken the trouble to read up to this sentence, we promise to leave no stone unturned to make this preface as lively and entertaining as possible. For your reading pleasure, here is a nice story with a picture thrown in for good measure. Enjoy!

Once upon a time, there were six blind men. The blind men wished to know what an elephant looked like. They took a trip to the forest and with the help of their guide found a tame elephant. The first blind man walked into the broadside of the elephant and bumped his head. He declared that the elephant was like a wall. The second one grabbed the elephant's tusk and said it felt like a spear. The next blind man felt the trunk of the elephant and was sure that elephants were similar to snakes. The fourth blind man hugged the elephant's leg and declared the elephant was like a tree. The next one caught the ear and said this is definitely like a fan. The last blind man felt the tail and said this sure feels like a rope. Thus the six blind men all perceived one aspect of the elephant and were each right in their own way, but none of them knew what the whole elephant really looked like.

Oftentimes, the market poses itself as the elephant. There are people who say that predicting the market is like predicting the weather, because you can do well in the short term, but where the market will be in the long run is anybody's guess. We have also heard from others that predicting the market short term is a sure way to burn your fingers. "Invest for the long haul" is their mantra. Some will assert that the markets are efficient, and yet some others would tell you that it is possible to make extraordinary returns. While some swear by technical analysis, there are some others, the so-called fundamentalists, who staunchly claim it to be a voodoo science. Multiple valuation models for equities like the dividend discount model, relative valuation models, and the Merton model (treating equity as an option on firm value) all exist side by side, each being relevant at different times for different stocks. Deep theories from various disciplines like physics, statistics, control theory, graph theory, game theory, signal processing, probability, and geometry have all been applied to explain different aspects of market behavior.

It seems as if the market is willing to accommodate a wide range of sometimes opposing belief systems. If we are to make any sense of this smorgasbord of opinions on the market, we would be well advised to draw comfort from the story of the six blind men and the elephant. Under these circumstances, if the reader goes away with a few more perspectives on the market elephant, the author would consider his job well done.

Acknowledgments

All of what is in the book has resulted from the people who have touched my life, and I wish to acknowledge them. First, I thank my parents for raising me in an atmosphere of high expectations: my dad, for his keen interest in this project and for suggesting the term *stogistics*, and my mom, for her unwavering confidence in my abilities. I also thank my in-laws for being so gracious and generous with their support and for sharing in the excitement of the whole process.

I greatly thank friends Jaya Kannan and Kasturi Kannan for their thoughtful gestures and good cheer during the writing process. Thanks to my brother, brother-in-law, and their spouses—Chintu, Hema, Ganesh, and Annie—for their kind and timely enquiries on the status of the writing. It definitely served as a gentle reminder at times when I was lagging behind schedule.

I owe a deep debt of gratitude to my teachers not only for the gift of knowledge but also for inculcating a joy for the learning process, especially Professor Narasimha Murthy, Professor Earl Barnes, and Professor Robert V. Kohn, all of whom I have enjoyed the privilege of working with closely.

The contents of Chapters 11 and 12 are an outcome of the many discussions with Professor Robert V. Kohn (Courant Institute of Mathematics, New York University). The risk arbitrage data were provided by Jason Dahl. The cartoon illustrations done by Tom Kerr are better than I could ever imagine. I thank all of them.

Professors Marco Avellaneda (Courant Institute of Mathematics), Robert V. Kohn (Courant Institute of Mathematics), Kumar Venkataraman (Cox School of Business Southern Methodist University), and professionals Paul Crowley, Steve Evans, Brooke Allen, Jason Dahl, Bud Kroll, and Ajay Junnarkar agreed to review draft versions of the manuscript. Many thanks to all of them. All mistakes that have been overlooked are mine.

I thank my editor, Dave Pugh, for ensuring that the process of writing was a smooth and pleasurable one. Also, thanks to the staff at John Wiley, including Debra Englander for their assistance.

I apologize for any persons left out due to my absentmindedness. Please accept my unspoken thanks.

Last, but most importantly, I wish to thank my wife, Lalitha, for all the wonderful years, for teaching me regularization and being able to share in the excitement of new ideas. Also, thanks to Anjali and Sandhya without whose help the project would have concluded a lot sooner, but would have been no fun at all. You make it all worth it.

Background Material

Introduction

We start at the very beginning (a very good place to start). We begin with the CAPM model.

THE CAPM MODEL

CAPM is an acronym for the Capital Asset Pricing Model. It was originally proposed by William T. Sharpe. The impact that the model has made in the area of finance is readily evident in the prevalent use of the word *beta*. In contemporary finance vernacular, beta is not just a nondescript Greek letter, but its use carries with it all the import and implications of its CAPM definition.

Along with the idea of beta, CAPM also served to formalize the notion of a market portfolio. A market portfolio in CAPM terms is a portfolio of assets that acts as a proxy for the market. Although practical versions of market portfolios in the form of market averages were already prevalent at the time the theory was proposed, CAPM definitely served to underscore the significance of these market averages.

Armed with the twin ideas of market portfolio and beta, CAPM attempts to explain asset returns as an aggregate sum of component returns. In other words, the return on an asset in the CAPM framework can be separated into two components. One is the market or systematic component, and the other is the residual or nonsystematic component. More precisely, if r_p is the return on the asset, r_m is the return on the market portfolio, and the beta of the asset is denoted as β, the formula showing the relationship that achieves the separation of the returns is given as

$$r_p = \beta r_m + \theta_p \qquad (1.1)$$

Equation 1.1 is also often referred to as the security market line (SML). Note that in the formula, βr_m is the market or systematic component of the return. β serves as a leverage number of the asset return over the market return. For instance, if the beta of the asset happens to be 3.0 and the market moves 1 percent, the systematic component of the asset return is now 3.0 percent. This idea is readily apparent when the SML is viewed in geometrical terms in Figure 1.1. It may also be deduced from the figure that β is indeed the slope of the SML.

θ_p in the CAPM equation is the residual component or residual return on the portfolio. It is the portion of the asset return that is not explainable by the market return. The consensus expectation on the residual component is assumed to be zero.

Having established the separation of asset returns into two components, CAPM then proceeds to elaborate on a key assumption made with respect to the relationship between them. The assertion of the model is that the market component and residual component are uncorrelated. Now, many a scholarly discussion on the import of these assumptions has been conducted and a lot of ink used up on the significance of the CAPM model since its introduction. Summaries of those discussions may be found in the references provided at the end of the chapter. However, for our purposes, the preceding introduction explaining the notion of beta and its role in the determination of asset returns will suffice.

Given that knowledge of the beta of an asset is greatly valuable in the CAPM context, let us discuss briefly how we can go about estimating its value. Notice that beta is actually the slope of the SML. Therefore, beta may be estimated as the slope of the regression line between market returns and the asset returns. Applying the standard regression formula for the estimation of the slope we have

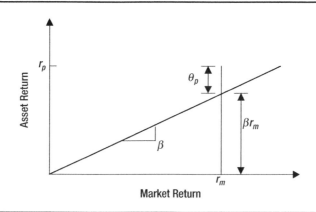

FIGURE 1.1 The Security Market Line.

$$\beta = \frac{\text{cov}(r_p r_m)}{\text{var}(r_m)} \qquad (1.2)$$

that is, beta is the covariance between the asset and market returns divided by the variance of the market returns.

To see the typical range of values that the beta of an asset is likely to assume in practice, we remind ourselves of an oft-quoted adage about the markets, "A rising tide raises all boats." The statement indicates that when the market goes up, we can typically expect the price of all securities to go up with it. Thus, a positive return for the market usually implies a positive return for the asset, that is, the sum of the market component and the residual component is positive. If the residual component of the asset return is small, as we expect it to be, then the positive return in the asset is explained almost completely by its market component. Therefore, a positive return in the market portfolio and the asset implies a positive market component of the return and, by implication, a positive value for beta. Therefore, we can expect all assets to typically have positive values for their betas.

MARKET NEUTRAL STRATEGY

Having discussed CAPM, we now have the required machinery to define *market neutral strategies*: They are strategies that are neutral to market returns, that is, the return from the strategy is uncorrelated with the market return. Regardless of whether the market goes up or down, in good times and bad the market neutral strategy performs in a steady manner, and results are typically achieved with a lower volatility. This desired outcome is achieved by trading market neutral portfolios. Let us therefore define what we mean by a market neutral portfolio.

In the CAPM context, *market neutral portfolios* may be defined as portfolios whose beta is zero. To examine the implications, let us apply a beta value of zero to the equation for the SML. It is easy to see that the return on the portfolio ceases to have a market component and is completely determined by θ_p, the residual component. The residual component by the CAPM assumption happens to be uncorrelated with market returns, and the portfolio return is therefore *neutral* to the market. Thus, a zero beta portfolio qualifies as a market neutral portfolio.

In working with market neutral portfolios, the trader can now focus on forecasting and trading the residual returns. Since the consensus expectation or mean on the residual return is zero, it is reasonable to expect a strong mean-reverting behavior (value oscillates back and forth about the mean value) of the residual time series.[1] This mean-reverting behavior can then be exploited in the process of return prediction, leading to trading signals that constitute the trading strategy.

Let us now examine how we can construct market neutral portfolios and what we should expect by way of the composition of such portfolios. Consider a portfolio that is composed of strictly long positions in assets. We expect that beta of the assets to be positive. Then positive returns in the market result in a positive return for the assets and thereby a positive return for the portfolio. This would, of course, imply a positive beta for the portfolio. By a similar argument it is easy to see that a portfolio composed of strictly short positions is likely to have a negative beta. So, how do we construct a zero beta portfolio, using securities with positive betas? This would not be possible without holding both long and short positions on different assets in the portfolio. We therefore conclude that one can typically expect a zero beta portfolio to comprise both long and short positions. For this reason, these portfolios are also called long–short portfolios. Another artifact of long–short portfolios is that the dollar proceeds from the short sale are used almost entirely to establish the long position, that is, the net dollar value of holdings is close to zero. Not surprisingly, zero beta portfolios are also sometimes referred to as *dollar neutral portfolios*.

Example

Let us consider two portfolios A and B, with positive betas β_A and β_B and with returns r_A and r_B

$$r_A = \beta_A r_m + \theta_A \qquad (1.3)$$
$$r_B = \beta_B r_m + \theta_B$$

We now construct a portfolio AB, by taking a short position on r units of portfolio A and a long position on one unit of portfolio B. The return on this portfolio is given as $r_{AB} = -r.r_A + r_B$. Substituting for the values of r_A and r_B, we have

$$r_{AB} = (-r\beta_A + \beta_B).r_m + (-r.\theta_A + \theta_B) \qquad (1.4)$$

---

[1]The assertion of CAPM that the expected value of residual return is zero is rather strong. It has been discussed extensively in academic literature as to whether this prediction of CAPM is indeed observable. It is therefore recommended that we explicitly verify the mean-reverting behavior of the spread time series. In later chapters we will discuss methods to statistically check for mean-reverting behavior.

Thus, the combined portfolio has an effective beta of $-r\beta_A + \beta_B$. This value becomes zero, when $r = \beta_B/\beta_A$. Thus, by a judicious choice of the value of r in the long–short portfolio we have created a market neutral portfolio.

COCKTAIL CORNER

In cocktail situations involving investment professionals, it is fairly common to hear the terms *long–short, market neutral,* and *dollar neutral investing* bandied about. Very often they are assumed to mean the same thing. Actually, that need not be the case. You could be long–short and dollar neutral but still have a nonzero beta to the market. In which case you have a nonzero market component in the portfolio return and therefore are not market neutral.

If you ever encountered such a situation, you could smile to yourself. Tempting as it might be, I strongly urge that you restrain yourself. But, of course, if you are looking to be anointed the "resident nerd," you could go ahead and launch into an exhaustive explanation of the subtle differences to people with cocktails in hand not particularly looking for a lesson in precise terminology.

PAIRS TRADING

Pairs trading is a market neutral strategy in its most primitive form. The market neutral portfolios are constructed using just two securities, consisting of a long position in one security and a short position in the other, in a predetermined ratio. At any given time, the portfolio is associated with a quantity called the *spread*. This quantity is computed using the quoted prices of the two securities and forms a time series. The spread is in some ways related to the residual return component of the return already discussed. Pairs trading involves putting on positions when the spread is substantially away from its mean value, with the expectation that the spread will revert back. The positions are then reversed upon convergence. In this book, we will look at two versions of pairs trading in the equity markets; namely, statistical arbitrage pairs and risk arbitrage pairs.

Statistical arbitrage pairs trading is based on the idea of relative pricing. The underlying premise in relative pricing is that stocks with similar characteristics must be priced more or less the same. The spread in this case may be thought of as the degree of mutual mispricing. The greater the spread, the higher the magnitude of mispricing and greater the profit potential.

The strategy involves assuming a long–short position when the spread is substantially away from the mean. This is done with the expectation that the mispricing is likely to correct itself. The position is then reversed and profits made when the spread reverts back. This brings up several questions: How do we go about calculating the spread? How do we identify stock pairs for which such a strategy would work? What value do we use for the ratio in the construction of the pairs portfolio? When can we say that the spread has substantially diverged from the mean? We will address these questions and provide some quantitative tools to answer them.

Risk arbitrage pairs occur in the context of a merger between two companies. The terms of the merger agreement establish a strict parity relationship between the values of the stocks of the two firms involved. The spread in this case is the magnitude of the deviation from the defined parity relationship. If the merger between the two companies is deemed a certainty, then the stock prices of the two firms must satisfy the parity relationship, and the spread between them will be zero. However, there is usually a certain level of uncertainty on the successful completion of a merger after the announcement, because of various reasons like antitrust regulatory issues, proxy battles, competing bidders, and the like. This uncertainty is reflected in a nonzero value for the spread. Risk arbitrage involves taking on this uncertainty as risk and capturing the spread value as profits. Thus, unlike the case of statistical arbitrage pairs, which is based on valuation considerations, risk arbitrage trade is based strictly on a parity relationship between the prices of the two stocks.

The typical modus operandi is as follows. Let us call the acquiring firm the "bidder" and the acquired firm the "target." On the eve of merger announcement, the bidder shares are sold short and the target shares are bought. The position is then unwound on completion of the merger. The spread on merger completion is usually lower than when it was put on. The realized profit is the difference between the two spreads. In this book, we discuss how the ratio is determined based on the details of the merger agreement. We will develop a model for the spread dynamics that can be used to answer questions like, "What is the market expectation on the odds of merger completion?" We shall also demonstrate how the model may be used for risk management. Additionally, we will focus on trade timing and provide some quantitative tools for the process.

OUTLINE

The book provides an overview of two different versions of pairs trading in the equity markets. The first version is based on the idea of relative valuation and is called *statistical arbitrage pairs trading*. The second involves pairs trading that arises in the context of mergers and is called *risk arbitrage*. Even though they are commonly called arbitrage strategies in the industry, they are by no means risk-free. In this book we take an in-depth look at the various aspects of these strategies and provide quantitative tools to assist in their analysis.

I must also quickly point out at this juncture that the methodologies discussed in the book are not by any measure to be construed as the only way to trade pairs because, to put it proverbially, there is more than one way to skin a cat. We do, however, strive to present a compelling point of view attempting to integrate theory and practice. The book is by no means meant to be a guarantee for success in pairs trading. However, it provides a framework and insights on applying rigorous analysis to trading pairs in the equity markets.

The book is in three parts. In the first part, we present preliminary material on some key topics. We concede that there are books entirely devoted to each of the topics addressed, and the coverage of the topics here is not exhaustive. However, the discussion sets the context for the rest of the book and helps familiarize the reader with some important ideas. It also introduces some notation and definitions. The second part is devoted to statistical arbitrage pairs, and the third part is on risk arbitrage.

The book assumes some knowledge on the part of the reader of algebra, probability theory, and calculus. Nevertheless, we have strived to make the material accessible and the reader could choose to pick up the background along the way. As a refresher, the appendix at the end of this chapter lists the basic probability formulas that the reader can expect to encounter in the course of reading the book.

In terms of the sequence of chapters, we highly recommend that readers familiarize themselves with the chapters on time series and multifactor models before getting on to statistical arbitrage pairs, as those ideas and technical terms are referenced quite frequently in the course of the discussions. Concepts from Chapter 4, on Kalman filtering, are used in Chapter 12, related to smoothing risk arbitrage spreads. Other than the preceding dependencies, the rest of the material is mostly self-contained.

AUDIENCE

This book is written to appeal to a broad audience spanning students, practitioners, and self-study enthusiasts. It is written in an easy reading style, first presenting the broad ideas and concepts and subsequently delving into the details. The idea is to provide readers with the flexibility to revisit aspects of the details on their own timetable. To further facilitate this, a bullet summary highlighting the key points is provided at the end of every chapter. The book could serve as a reference text for students pursuing a degree in mathematical finance or be used as part of an advanced course for MBA students. Also, the topics addressed in the book would be of keen interest not only to academicians but also to traders and quantitative analysts in hedge funds and brokerage houses.

The background material in Part 1 provides a primer on various subjects that are drawn on in the course of the analysis. The background material and the analysis methodology appear as a recurring theme in strategy analysis and are generally applicable to other asset classes as well. Given this and the easy readable style of the book, we hope that this book serves as a reference for investment professionals.

SUMMARY

- The CAPM model helps separate out portfolio returns into a market component and a residual component.
- Portfolios with a zero market component are called market neutral portfolios.
- Market neutral strategies involve the trading of market neutral portfolios, and the returns generated by such strategies are uncorrelated with the market.
- Pairs trading is a genre of market neutral strategies in which a portfolio has only two assets.

■ In the book, we will discuss two classes of pairs trading strategies; namely, risk arbitrage and statistical arbitrage.

FURTHER READING MATERIAL

CAPM

Elton, Edwin J. and Martin J. Gruber. *Modern Portfolio Theory and Investment Analysis*, 4th Edition. (New York: John Wiley & Sons, Inc., 1991).
Fama, Eugene F. and Kenneth R. French. "The Cross-Section of Expected Stock Returns." *Journal of Finance* 47, no. 2 (June 1992): 427–465.

Market Neutral Strategies

Nicholas, Joseph G. *Market Neutral Investing: Long/Short Hedge Fund Strategies.* (New York: Bloomberg Press, 2000).

APPENDIX

Below are a few formulas on random variables that we are likely to encounter throughout the book.

DEFINITIONS

Let X, Y, and Z be random variables. Let $(x_1, y_1, z_1),(x_2, y_2, z_2),...,(x_N, y_N, z_N)$ be N realization 3-tuples for these random variables.

Mean

- The mean or expected value of X is denoted by $E[X] = \mu_x$.
- The estimated value of the mean of a random variable is known as the average.
- The formula for the average is $x_{avg} = \frac{1}{N}\sum_{i=1}^{N} x_i$.

Variance

- The variance of X is $var(X) = E\left[(x - \mu_x)^2\right]$.
- The estimated value of the square root of variance is the familiar standard deviation.
- Its value is calculated using the formula $x_{stddev} = \sqrt{\frac{1}{N}\sum_{i=1}^{N}(x_i - x_{avg})^2}$.

Covariance

- The covariance between X and Y is denoted as
$$cov(X, Y) = E\left[(x - \mu_x)(y - \mu_y)\right].$$
- An estimation of the covariance may be calculated using the formula
$$\frac{1}{N}\sum_{i=1}^{N}(x_i - x_{avg})(y_i - y_{avg}).$$

Correlation

- The correlation between X and Y is $corr(X, Y) = \dfrac{cov(X, Y)}{\sqrt{var(X)\,var(Y)}}$
- The formula for the estimate of correlation is given as
$$\frac{\frac{1}{N}\sum_{i=1}^{N}(x_i - x_{avg})(y_i - y_{avg})}{\left(X_{stddev}\right)\left(Y_{stddev}\right)}$$

- The correlation between any two random variables is always a value between +1 and –1.
- Every random variable is perfectly correlated with itself, that is, the correlation is 1.0.
- Two random variables are said to be uncorrelated when the correlation between them is 0.

FORMULAS

If α, β are nonrandom numbers, then the following formulas hold:

$E[\alpha X + \beta Y] = \alpha E[X] + \beta E[Y]$

$\text{var}(\alpha X + \beta) = \alpha^2 \, \text{var}(X)$

$\text{var}(X + Y) = \text{var}(X) + \text{var}(Y) + 2\text{cov}(X, Y)$

$\text{var}(X - Y) = \text{var}(X) + \text{var}(Y) - 2\text{cov}(X, Y)$

$\text{cov}(\alpha X, \beta Y) = \alpha \beta \text{cov}(X, Y)$

$\text{cov}(X, Y + Z) = \text{cov}(X, Y) + \text{cov}(X, Z)$

$\text{corr}(\alpha X, \beta Y) = \text{corr}(X, Y)$

CHAPTER 2

Time Series

OVERVIEW

A time series is a sequence of values measured over time. These values may be derived from a fixed deterministic formula, in which case they are referred to as a deterministic time series. Alternately, the value may be obtained by drawing a sample from a probability distribution, in which case they may be termed as probabilistic or stochastic time series. In this chapter, we will focus on stochastic time series.

Now, if the value at each instance in a stochastic time series is drawn from a probability distribution, how is it different from repeated drawings from a probability distribution? The added twist is that the probability distributions used for the drawings can themselves vary with time. The formal specification prescribing ways in which the distributions could vary with time and the discipline of analyzing stochastic time series was pioneered and popularized by Nobert Weiner.[1] For this reason, the subject area is also referred to at times as Weiner filtering.

In the early days of Weiner filtering, the ideas were in theorem form, and to use them in practical applications one had to work through the rigorous mathematical definitions and theorems. Along came George Box and Gwilym Jenkins in the early 1970s, who formulated the application of Weiner filtering concepts into a recipe-like format. Their step-by-step prescription to the process of model building not only had great intuitive appeal but also managed to transform what was considered an esoteric science into a robust engineering discipline. The approach could now be readily applied to forecasting problems. The methodology gained instant popularity with time series analysts and has become the staple by far for the analysis of sto-

---

[1] Nobert Weiner is also credited with coining the word *cybernetics*, the shortened version of which is the ubiquitous *cyber*, which has by usage become a prefix for a lot of terms associated with the Internet.

chastic time series. Fittingly, their methodology for time series forecasting is referred to as the Box-Jenkins approach. In this chapter, we will describe the Box-Jenkins approach. Instead of doing this by definition, we will attempt to do this by way of construction and examples.

We begin by introducing some basic notation. Throughout the chapter the value of a time series at time t is denoted as y_t. It then follows that the general time series is the set of values y_t, $t = 0, 1, 2, 3...T$. We denote this as y_t.

AUTOCORRELATION

Let us begin the discussion by introducing the notion of the autocorrelation. Given a stochastic time series, the first question one tends to ask in the process of analysis is, "Is there a relationship between the value now and the value observed one time step in the past?" We can choose to answer the question by measuring the correlation between the time series values one time interval apart. The strength of the (linear) relationship is reflected in the correlation number. And what about the relationship of the current value to the value two time steps in the past? What about three time steps in the past? The question seems to repeat itself naturally for the whole range of time steps. The answer to these questions, spanning the entire range of time steps, could very well be the autocorrelation function.

The autocorrelation function is the plot of the correlation between values in the time series based on the time interval between them. The x-axis denotes the length of the time lag between the current value and the value in the past. The y-axis value for a time lag τ, $(x = \tau)$ is the correlation between the values in the time series τ time units apart. This correlation is estimated using the formula

$$\hat{\rho}(\tau) = \frac{\frac{1}{T} \sum_{t=\tau+1}^{T} [y_t - \overline{y}][y_{t-\tau} - \overline{y}]}{\frac{1}{T} \sum_{t=1}^{T} (y_t - \overline{y})^2} \tag{2.1}$$

where $\overline{y}$ is the calculated average of variable y.

The plot of the estimated correlation against time intervals forms an estimation of the autocorrelation function, called the *correlogram*. It serves as a proxy for the autocorrelation function of the time series.

We shall see in the ensuing discussions that the autocorrelation function serves as a signature or fingerprint for a time series and plays a key role in characterizing various cases of the time series that we describe in the following sections.

TIME SERIES MODELS

The approach we will adopt in the description of time series models is to start with the special cases and eventually build up to the generalized version.

White Noise

The white noise is the simplest case of a probabilistic time series. It is constructed by drawing a value from a normal distribution at each time instance. Furthermore, the parameters of the normal distribution are fixed and do not change with time. Thus, in this case, the time series is equivalent to drawing samples repeatedly from a probability distribution. If we denote the value from the drawing at time t as ε_t, the value of the time series at time t is then $y_t = \varepsilon_t$.

Note that there is no special requirement in the definition of white noise that the invariant distribution be a normal or Gaussian distribution. This is, however, the most widely used version of white noise in practice and is referred to as *Gaussian white noise*.

A plot of a white noise series is shown in Figure 2.1a. The correlogram for that time series is calculated as is shown in Figure 2.1b. Note that at the lag value of zero, the correlation is unity; that is, every sample is perfectly correlated with itself. At all the other lag values the measured correlation is negligible. Let us see why that is. At all time steps, the values are drawn from identical independent normal distributions. It is also a fact that the correlation between independent random variables is zero; that is, they are uncorrelated. Therefore, for a white noise series, the correlation between the values for all time intervals is zero, and this is reflected in the correlogram. But what is the genesis of the term *white noise*? It has to do with the Fourier transform of the autocorrelation function. A discussion of that is a little beyond the scope of this introduction, so for that we direct the reader to other books written in the area, as noted in the reference section.

Let us now focus on the predictability of the white noise time series. The question we ask is as follows: Does knowledge of the past realization help in the prediction of the time series value in the next time instant? It does help to some extent. Knowledge of the past realization helps us to estimate the variance of the normal distribution. This enables us to arrive at some intelligent conclusions about the odds of the next realization of the time series being greater than or less than some value.

Summing up, in a white noise series, the variance of the value at each point in the series is the variance of the normal distribution used for drawing the white noise values. This distribution with a specific mean and variance is time invariant. Thus, a white noise series is a sequence of uncorrelated random variables with constant mean and variance.

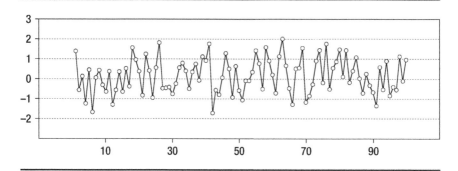

FIGURE 2.1A   White Noise Series.

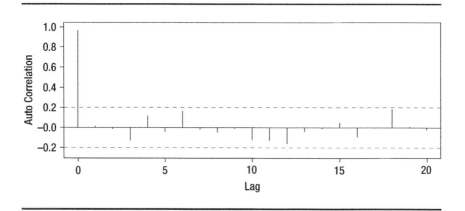

FIGURE 2.1B   White Noise ACF.

Moving Average Process (MA)

We now generate another time series from the white noise series above. The value y_t of this time series at time t is given by the rule

$$y_t = \varepsilon_t + \beta\varepsilon_{t-1} \tag{2.2}$$

In words, the time series value is the sum of the current white noise realization plus beta[2] times the white noise realization one time step ago. Note that

---

[2]Beta in this connotation is a nondescript Greek symbol denoting a constant and has no relationship to the CAPM model.

when $\beta = 0$, this is the same as the white noise series. In Figure 2.2a is a plot of a time series of this type. This specific time series was generated from the white noise sequence in Figure 2.1 using the formula $y_t = \varepsilon_t + 0.8\varepsilon_{t-1}$. The correlogram of the series is plotted in Figure 2.2b. In the correlogram, note that there is a steep drop in the value after $\tau = 1$. To see why that is, let us consider the time series values for the three consecutive time steps t, $t + 1$, and $t + 2$.

$$\begin{aligned} y_t &= \varepsilon_t + \beta\varepsilon_{t-1} \\ y_{t+1} &= \varepsilon_{t+1} + \beta\varepsilon_t \\ y_{t+2} &= \varepsilon_{t+2} + \beta\varepsilon_{t+1} \end{aligned} \qquad\qquad (2.3)$$

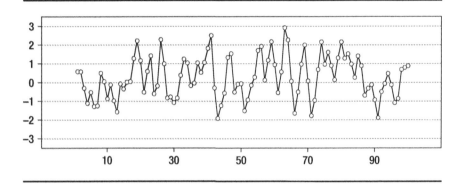

FIGURE 2.2A MA(1) Series.

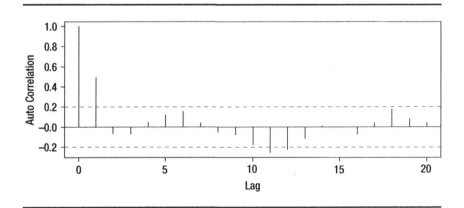

FIGURE 2.2B MA(1) Series ACF.

Observe that the values one time interval apart ($\tau = 1$) have in their terms one common white noise realization value (albeit with different coefficients). Between y_t and y_{t+1} the common white noise realization is ε_t. Similarly, between y_{t+1} and y_{t+2} there is ε_{t+1}. Because of this, we expect there to be some correlation between them.

However, between y_t and y_{t+2}, values two time intervals apart ($\tau = 2$), we have no common white noise realizations. They are independent drawings from normal distributions and are therefore uncorrelated (correlation = 0). Thus, after exhibiting strong correlation after one time step, the correlation goes to zero from the next time step onward. This would explain the steep drop in correlation after $\tau = 1$.

To examine the predictability of this time series, we again ask the same question: Does knowledge of the past realization help in the prediction of the next time series value? The answer here is a resounding yes. At time step t we know what the white noise realization was at time step $t - 1$. Thus our prediction for time step t would be a value that is normally distributed with the mean, $y_t^{\text{pred}} = \beta\varepsilon_{t-1}$. The variance of the predicted value would be the variance of the ε_t, which is same as the variance of the white noise used to construct the time series. Since these values are based on the condition that we know the past realization of the time series, they are called the *conditional mean* and the *conditional variance* of the time series. To conclude, knowledge of the past definitely helps in the prediction of time series.

Summing up, the preceding series was constructed using a linear combination (moving average) of white noise realizations. The series is therefore called a moving average (MA) series. Also, because we used the current value and one lagged value of the white noise series, the series qualifies as a first-order moving average process, denoted as MA(1). This idea is easily generalized to a series where the value is constructed using q lagged values of white noise realizations.

$$y_t = \varepsilon_t + \beta_1\varepsilon_{t-1} + \beta_2\varepsilon_{t-2} + ... + \beta_q\varepsilon_{t-q} \tag{2.4}$$

Such a series is called the moving average series of order q or an MA(q) series.

Autoregressive Process (AR)

In the previous example we had constructed a time series by taking a linear combination of a finite number of past white noise realizations. In this section we will construct the series using a linear combination of infinite past values of the white noise realization. In practice, though, infinity is approximated by taking a very large number of values. A question that immediately pops to mind is that if we add an infinite sequence of numbers, will the sum not go to infinity? In some instances it might go to infinity. There are, however, cases where the sum of an infinite sequence of numbers is actually a finite value.[3] Let us denote the value of the time series at instant t as

$$y_t = \varepsilon_t + \alpha\varepsilon_{t-1} + \alpha^2\varepsilon_{t-2} + ... \tag{2.5}$$

The infinite moving average representation above is called the MA(∞) representation. To simplify Equation 2.5, consider the value of the time series at $t - 1$. It is given as

$$y_{t-1} = \varepsilon_{t-1} + \alpha\varepsilon_{t-2} + \alpha^2\varepsilon_{t-3} + ... \tag{2.6}$$

Examining the two equations, note that we can write y_t in terms of y_{t-1} as follows:

$$y_t = \alpha y_{t-1} + \varepsilon_t \tag{2.7}$$

In words, the value at time t is alpha times the value at time $t - 1$ plus a white noise term. Note that alpha may be viewed as the slope of the regression between two consecutive values of the time series. Since the next value in the time series is obtained by multiplying the past value with the slope of the regression, it is called an autoregressive (AR) series. Figure 2.3a is the plot of the AR time series, generated using the white noise values seen in Figure 2.1.

The corresponding correlogram is shown in Figure 2.3b. Notice that the correlation values fall off gradually with increasing lag values; that is, there is not much of a sharp drop. To get an insight into why that is, let us apply the same kind of reasoning as we did for the MA model. Every time step has in it additive terms comprising all the previous white noise realizations. Therefore, there will always be white noise realizations that are common between two values of the time series however far apart they may be. Naturally, we can expect there to be some correlation between any two values in the time series regardless of the time interval between them. It is therefore not surprising that the correlation exhibits a slow decay.

To answer the predictability question, here, too, as in the moving average case, knowledge of the past values of the time series is helpful in predicting what the next value is likely to be. In this case we have $y_t^{\text{pred}} = \alpha y_{t-1}$. The conditional variance of the predicted value would be the variance of the ε_t, which is same as the variance of the white noise used to construct the time series.

The one-step autoregressive series may be extended to an autoregressive (AR) series of order p, denoted as AR(p). The value at time t is given as

---

[3]We touch upon this topic very briefly in the appendix. However, for a full-blown discussion on stability analysis, we recommend that the reader follow up with the references.

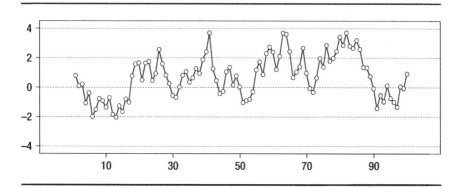

FIGURE 2.3A   AR(1) Series.

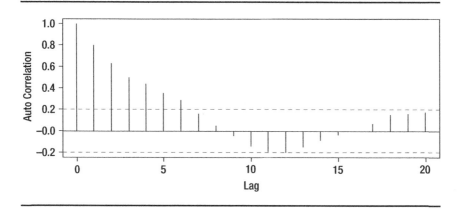

FIGURE 2.3B   AR(1) Series ACF.

$$y_t = \varepsilon_t + \alpha_1 y_{t-1} + \alpha_2 y_{t-2} + ... + \alpha_p y_{t-p} \tag{2.8}$$

It is, however, important to bear in mind that the generalized AR series is generated from a white noise series using linear combinations of past realizations.

The General ARMA Process

The AR(p) and MA(q) models can be mixed to form an ARMA(p, q) model. By extrapolation it is easy to see that the generation rule for an ARMA (p, q) process is given as

$$y_t = \left[\alpha_1 y_{t-1} + \alpha_2 y_{t-2} + \ldots + \alpha_p y_{t-p}\right] + \tag{2.9}$$

$$+ \left[\varepsilon_t + \beta_1 \varepsilon_{t-1} + \beta_2 \varepsilon_{t-2} + \ldots + \beta_q \varepsilon_{t-q}\right]$$

We once again underscore the main point (hoping to drive it home) by quoting our constant refrain pertaining to Weiner filtering: *The preceding models are all constructed using a linear combination of past values of the white noise series.* An important consequence of that fact is that the sum of two independent ARMA series is also ARMA.

The Random Walk Process

An important and special ARMA series that merits discussion is the random walk. The random walk has been studied extensively by scientists from various disciplines. Phenomena ranging from the movement of molecules to fluctuations of stock prices have been modeled as random walks. Let us therefore discuss this in some detail.

A random walk is an AR(1) series with $\alpha = 1$. From the definition of an AR series given, the value of the time series at time t is therefore

$$y_t = \varepsilon_t + \varepsilon_{t-1} + \varepsilon_{t-2} + \ldots = \varepsilon_t + y_{t-1} \tag{2.10}$$

In words, the random walk is essentially a simple sum of all the white noise realizations up to the current time. The AR representation provides an alternate way to look at the random walk. It is the value of the time series one time step ago plus the white noise realization at the current time step. The white noise realization at the current time step in the case of the random walk is known as the *innovation*. Figure 2.4 is a picture of the random walk generated using the white noise series in Figure 2.1.

Let us now begin to examine some properties of the random walk. What do we expect the variance of the random walk to be at time t? Applying the formulas from the appendix in Chapter 1 on the MA(∞) (infinity) representation of the random walk, along with the fact that white noise drawings are uncorrelated, we have

$$\mathrm{var}(y_t) = \mathrm{var}(\varepsilon_t) + \mathrm{var}(\varepsilon_{t-1}) + \mathrm{var}(\varepsilon_{t-2}) + \cdots + \mathrm{var}(\varepsilon_1) \tag{2.11}$$

Since these random white noise drawings all have the same variance, the variance of the random walk at any time t is clearly

$$\mathrm{var}(y_t) = t\,\mathrm{var}(\varepsilon_t) \tag{2.12}$$

Note that in this case the variance depends on the time instant, and it increases linearly with time t. (If the variance increases linearly with t, then the

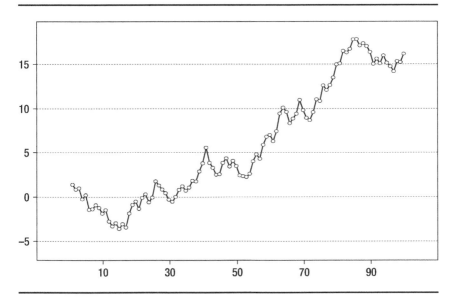

FIGURE 2.4 Random Walk Series.

standard deviation increases linearly with $\sqrt{t}$). In this case, unlike all the previous cases, the variance increases monotonically with time; that is, the values are capable of moving to extremes with the passage of time. Also, the statistical parameters like the unconditional mean and variance are not time invariant, or *stationary*. The series is therefore called a *nonstationary* time series.

The correlation between a value and its immediate lagging value is 1. Our prediction for the next time step would then be a value with mean equal to the current time step; that is, $y_t^{\text{pred}} = y_{t-1}$. The variance, of course, is the variance of the white noise realizations. As a matter of fact, our prediction for any number of time steps would be a distribution whose mean is the current value of the series. However, because the variance increases linearly with time, the error in our prediction progressively increases with the number of time steps.

Of the different time series reviewed so far, the random walk is the only series in which the prediction of the mean value for the next time step is the current value. Such series where the expected value at the next time step are the value at the current time step are known as *martingales*. The random walk qualifies as a martingale.

The random walk also exhibits a strong trending behavior. Let us examine that statement by contrasting the behavior of the random walk with other time series. The other time series tend to oscillate about the mean of the series; that is, they exhibit *mean reversion*. To see what we mean, we suggest that the reader examine the time series plots and see how many times the different time series cross the mean (zero in this case). It is easy to see that the random walk has the least number of zero crossings. Even though the increments to the series at each time instance have equal odds of being positive or negative, it is not uncommon for the random walk series to stay positive (or negative) during the entire time.

FORECASTING

Having discussed the stochastic time series models, let us now direct our attention to the problem of forecasting. The classical forecasting problem may be stated as follows: We are given historical time series data with values up to the current time. We are required to predict the value of the next time step value as closely as possible. In the stochastic time series context, this means that we first identify the ARMA model that is most likely to have resulted in the data set and then use the estimated parameters of the model to forecast the next value of the time series.

Let us now formally lay down the steps involved in forecasting problems involving stochastic time series. The solution method is best described as a three-step process. The first step involves transforming the time series such that it is amenable to analysis. We call this the *preprocessing* step. The data are then analyzed for patterns that may clue us in on the dynamics of the time series. This means that we identify the ARMA model that is likely to have resulted in the data. This is the *analysis* step. Finally, we make our prediction in the *prediction* step. We now discuss each of the three steps in detail.

Preprocessing involves dealing with pesky issues like checking for missing values, weeding out bad data, eliminating outliers, and so forth. It may also involve transforming the time series to prepare it for analysis. A simple transformation may be to subtract the mean of the series. Other methods may involve creating a new time series by a functional transformation. The application of the logarithmic function to values of the given series prior to analysis is a good example. In the context of ARMA models, an important transformation technique that is frequently used is known as *differencing*. It is a process by which a new series is constructed by taking the difference between two consecutive values in the given series. Let us discuss the motivation for doing that. The ARMA model based forecasting is typically focused on the stationary time series. If we are given a series that is deemed nonstationary, differencing helps transform the nonstationary series into a stationary series. The output from the differencing operation may be viewed as the series of increments to the current value. Thus, analyzing the differenced output amounts to studying the changes in the values as opposed to the values themselves.

The next step is the analysis step. It involves identifying the ARMA model used to generate the given time series data. An ARMA model is completely identified when we are given the white noise series and the rule to generate the time series from the white noise realizations. Sometimes, the white noise series is implicit. The estimated ARMA parameters are, however, stated explicitly. But why should we try to fit an ARMA model to a given data set? The answer is simply that ARMA models provide an empirical explanation for the data without concerning themselves with theoretical justifications. This makes them readily applicable to a variety of situations. Also, the fact that ARMA models are empirical is not necessarily a bad thing, as insights from the model fitting exercise can be later used to construct a plausible theory.

Once the underlying ARMA model is identified, we can proceed to the prediction step. We use the model parameters to predict the next value in the series. This completes the forecasting exercise. As seen earlier in our discussion of the ARMA model, the prediction of the next time step value is rather straightforward once the model is identified. Therefore, insofar as forecasting is concerned, identifying the correct model is key to obtaining a good forecast. Not surprisingly, a good portion of the field of time series analysis is focused on model identification.

GOODNESS OF FIT VERSUS BIAS

We noted that identifying the right model is key to obtaining a good forecast. There are quite a few software packages[4] that estimate parameter values for ARMA models. While they are based on a variety of approaches, the basic underlying theme in all of them remains the same; that is, the goal to find the most appropriate ARMA model. Note the use of the term *most appropriate*. Let us focus on what it actually means.

Intuitively, a model may be deemed appropriate based on the accuracy with which it is able to account for the given data set. Let us call the number that quantifies this accuracy the "goodness of fit" measure. An example of the goodness of fit measure is the least squares criterion, which is simply the sum of squares of the prediction error. Prediction error is defined as the difference between the actual observation and the value predicted by the model. The idea then is to find a model that minimizes the least squares

---

[4]Eviews, S-Plus, and SAS are some software packages that deal with time series modeling and forecasting.

criterion (sum of squared errors) for the given data. Another example of the goodness of fit measure is the maximum likelihood criterion. This is a number representative of the probability that the given data set was produced by a particular set of parameter values. The idea here is to find the parameters that maximize the probability, or the maximum likelihood criterion. Thus, the goodness of fit measure helps identify the best model for the given data set.

Of course, the preceding statement is not without caveats. Let us say that we are required to choose the best four-parameter model fitting the data. The goodness of fit criterion would do a wonderful job in helping us achieve that. It is, however, very likely that the best five-parameter model would have a better goodness of fit score. As a matter of fact, we can in all likelihood keep improving our goodness of fit score by increasing the number of explanatory variables. Therefore, using the goodness of fit score without reservation amounts to advocating the philosophy of the more the merrier for explanatory variables.

Is that necessarily a good thing? What happens when we apply the model to out-of-sample data? Will we get the same level of accuracy? To see the logic more clearly, let us discuss an extreme case where we fit 100 data points with a 100th-order polynomial (100 explanatory variables). With that, we can get an exact fit to the data and the best possible goodness of fit score ever. However, as a working model for prediction, it is probably not much use to us. Increasing the parameters indefinitely may result in a model that fits the current data set but performs poorly when used outside the current sample. Restating, we could say that our model with a large number of explanatory variables is hopelessly biased to the current data set. So, here is our dilemma: We can improve the goodness of fit by increasing the number of explanatory variables and run the risk of bias, or we can use few explanatory variables and possibly miss further reduction in forecast error. The question at this point is, "How do I know the point at which I have a reasonable goodness of fit, and at the same time know that I am not overly biased to the current data set?" The resolution of this forms the topic of discussion in the following section.

MODEL CHOICE

The model choice process attempts to achieve a trade-off between goodness of fit and bias. In order to decide whether to increase the number of explanatory variables, we pose the question, "Am I getting sufficient bang for the buck in terms of fit error reduction for the addition of the new explanatory variable?" If I am, then let us go with the additional variable; otherwise, we stick with the model at hand.

The Akaike information criterion (AIC) quantifies the preceding trade-off argument.[5] In general, every model with k parameters is associated with an AIC number as follows:

$$\text{AIC} = n \log\left(\sum_{i=1}^{n} \frac{e_i^2}{n} \right) + 2k \tag{2.13}$$

where e_i is the forecast error on the ith data point. Here, the first term represents the goodness of fit, and the second term is the bias. For every additional variable, the second term increases by a value of 2. However, when a variable is added, we expect the fit to improve and the variance of the forecast error to go down. If this reduction is more than 2, then the AIC value for the model with an additional variable will be lower, and we will have got our proverbial bang for the buck. If the value is higher, then the trade-off is not worth it, and we stick with the current model.

The rationale for the AIC formula and the quantitative value used for trade-off has a strong foundation in information theory and is far from arbitrary. Further follow-up material on this can be found in the reference section.

Example

The application of the AIC idea is illustrated in the following exercise. An AR(3) time series that was generated is shown in Figure 2.5a. AR models of various orders were fit to it and the AIC values calculated. The result is plotted in Figure 2.5b. The x-axis denotes the number of parameters in the AR

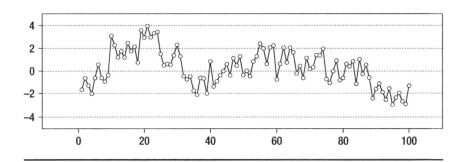

FIGURE 2.5A   AR(3) Series.

---

[5]AIC is but one of many cost functions. The Schwartz information criterion (SIC) and the Bayesian information criterion (BIC) are also popular.

BEFORE AIC: THE STATISTICIAN'S TORTURE

RAINING ON THE PARADE

If you ever happen to make a presentation involving data analysis, here is a situation that you might encounter. After all the preparation involving umpteen coffees, and bleary-eyed but vigorous mouse clicking at statistical packages as you present your forecasting model, there is a wise guy in the audience who quips, "I am sure I can fit any model to the degree of accuracy I want by adding a lot of variables. I do not see how your model is any good." While you would like to stare him down until he sulks and quietly leaves the room, more often than not the wise guy happens to be the boss. Unfortunately for you, more often than not he is also correct.

The key, however, is to be one up on the wise guy! Based on the preceding discussion you can now wax eloquently about the tug of war between goodness of fit and the evil of bias and how you have meticulously taken into account the effect of adding multiple variables in the forecasting model. Dazzle everyone with your slides on AIC calculations and top it off with an out-of-sample test.

If your presentation is close to end of fiscal year, you can chuckle to yourself about the bump in bonus you are likely to see due to this.

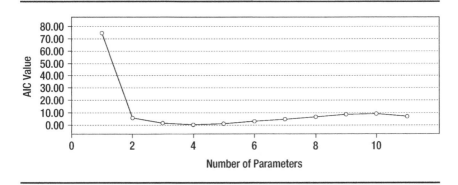

FIGURE 2.5B   AIC Plot.

model and the *y*-axis is the AIC value. Note that the AIC value registers a minimum at four parameters. This is three AR parameters and a constant value for the mean of the series. Using more parameters will result in a better goodness of fit but will not help in forecasting. In some instances, it might actually hurt the forecasting results.

MODELING STOCK PRICES

The model that is most commonly assumed for stock price movement is called a log-normal process; that is, the logarithm of the stock price is assumed to exhibit a random walk. Let us discuss the implications of such an assumption.

First, this says that the logarithm of the stock price is a martingale. This is to say that the observed price of a stock at the next time period is roughly equal to the price at the current time, give or take a few. That is definitely reasonable.

Next, let us examine the resulting time series when we difference the random walk. Differencing the random walk yields the increment to the random walk at each time step. The set of increments by definition are drawings from a normal distribution. But this is exactly how white noise is defined. Thus, differencing a random walk results in a white noise series. Also, bear in mind that the differencing output of the log-normal process (the difference in the logarithm of the prices) can be interpreted as the stock return.[6] Putting the two together, the implication of the log-normal assumption is that stock returns are essentially a white noise process. Let us look at the plausibility of this implication. Figure 2.6a is a plot of the logarithm of the price of GE (General Electric) over a 100-day period. The series is then differenced, yielding the differenced plot in Figure 2.6b. To quickly check the nature of differenced values (returns), we urge the reader to examine Figure 2.6d. It is a Q-Q plot of the returns versus the normal distribution. The closer the points are to the straight line, the more the actual distribution behaves like a normal distribution. The autocorrelation plot of the returns is depicted in Figure 2.6c. Note that the correlation values are negligible, signifying that an assumption of white noise for the differenced series in a random walk is definitely plausible.

Now, let us discuss the issues surrounding predictability in a random walk. We know that for a random walk the predicted value at the next time step is the value at the current time step. That is all fine, but the purpose of prediction is to make profits, and profits are made by correctly predicting the increment to the random walk in the next time period. However, because the random walk is a martingale, the mean value of the predicted increment is zero. The actual realized value of the increment is anybody's guess. Does the situation improve when we try to predict values two time steps ahead? Not very much really. The mean value of the predicted increment is still

---

[6] $\log(p_2) - \log(p_1) \approx \dfrac{p_2 - p_1}{p_1}$. Hence the difference in the logarithm may be construed to be the return.

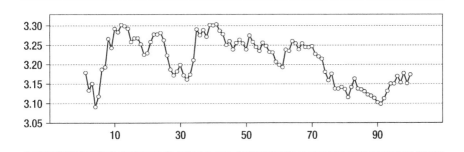

FIGURE 2.6A   GE Series.

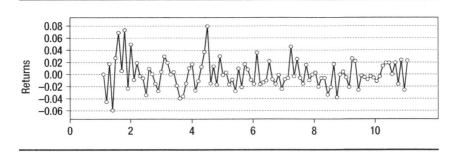

FIGURE 2.6B   Returns.

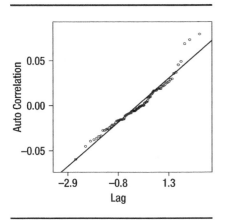

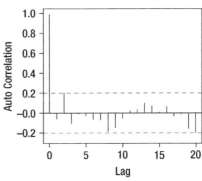

FIGURE 2.6C   GE Returns Q-Q Plot.   **FIGURE 2.6D**   GE Returns ACF.

zero. If anything, the variance of the normal distribution two time steps away increases, and the plausible range of values that the increment can assume actually increases, further increasing our prediction error. Therefore, knowing the past history of a random walk is not much help in predicting the forward-looking increments.

The situation is very different for stationary processes. Armed with the knowledge that stationary processes are mean reverting, one can predict the increment to be greater than or equal to the difference between the current value and the mean. The prediction is guaranteed to hold true at some point in the future realizations of the time series.

However, stock prices are modeled as a log-normal process, and that is definitely not stationary. So, where does that leave us in terms of making profits? Definitely not anywhere close to making money. The reader is probably wondering what the point of this whole chapter is. If the logarithm of stock prices is assumed to be random walk, there is no need to go at it in a roundabout way. Just say it is futile trying to predict stock returns and leave it at that. But all hope is not lost. We shall see in the later chapters that it may be possible to construct portfolios whose time series are actually stationary, and the returns for those portfolios are indeed predictable. Let us stop here with this teaser.

SUMMARY

- A time series is constructed by periodically drawing samples from probability distributions that vary with time.
- The white noise process is the most elementary form of time series and is generated by drawing samples from a fixed distribution at every time instance.
- ARMA time series are generated using fixed linear combinations of white noise realizations.
- Time series forecasting for ARMA processes involves deciphering the linear combination and the white noise sequence used to generate the given data and using it to predict the future values.
- A random walk process is the time series where the current value is a simple sum of all the white noise realizations up to the present time.
- A random walk is a nonstationary time series.
- Nonstationary time series are usually transformed to stationary time series using differencing.
- The logarithm of the stock price series is usually modeled as a random walk.

FURTHER READING MATERIAL

Time Series

Diebold, Francis X. *Elements of Forecasting.* (Cincinnati, Ohio: South Western College Publishing, 1998).

AIC

Akaike, H. "A New Look at Statistical Model Identification." *IEEE Transactions on Automatic Control* 19 (1974): 716–723.

APPENDIX

Lag 1 Correlation in a MA(1) Series

The variance of y_t can be calculated using the preceding formulas as

$$\text{var}(y_t) = \text{var}(\varepsilon_t + \beta\varepsilon_{t-1}) = \text{var}(\varepsilon_t) + \beta^2\,\text{var}(\varepsilon_{t-1}) + 2\beta\,\text{cov}(\varepsilon_t, \varepsilon_{t-1}) =$$

$$= (1 + \beta^2)\,\text{var}(\varepsilon_t)$$

$$\text{corr}(y_t, y_{t-1}) = \frac{E[y_t y_{t-1}]}{\sqrt{\text{var}(y_t)\,\text{var}(y_{t-1})}} = \frac{\beta E(\varepsilon_{t-1}^2)}{\sqrt{\text{var}(y_t)\,\text{var}(y_{t-1})}} =$$

$$= \frac{\beta\,\text{var}(\varepsilon_t)}{\text{var}(y_t)} = \frac{\beta}{1 + \beta^2}$$

Therefore, unlike the white noise series, this series has a nontrivial correlation structure.

Lag 1 Correlation in a AR(1) Series

The variance at each time instant is given as

$$\text{var}(y_t) = E(y_t^2) = (1 + \alpha^2 + \alpha^4 + \alpha^6 + \ldots)\,\text{var}(\varepsilon_t)$$

If $\alpha > 1$, the series explodes and the variance becomes infinity. However, when $\alpha > 1$, the variance can be calculated as the sum of an infinite geometric series and written as

$$\text{var}(y_t) = \frac{\text{var}(\varepsilon_t)}{1 - \alpha^2}$$

The covariance is given as

$$\text{cov}(y_t, y_{t-1}) = E[y_t y_{t-1}] = E[(\alpha y_{t-1} + \varepsilon_t)y_{t-1}] = \alpha\,\text{var}(y_t)$$

The correlation is therefore

$$\text{corr}\left(y_t, y_{t-1}\right) = \frac{\text{cov}\left(y_t, y_{t-1}\right)}{\text{var}\left(y_t\right)} = \frac{\alpha \, \text{var}\left(y_t\right)}{\text{var}\left(y_t\right)} = \alpha$$

Conditions under Which the Maximum Likelihood Is Equivalent to Minimizing Sum of Squares

The substitution of the logarithm of the likelihood criterion with the sum of the squared errors hinges on a key assumption. The assumption is that the errors follow a normal distribution with a zero mean. Based on this assumption, every error value may be assigned a probability of occurrence.

$$p\left(e_i\right) = \frac{1}{\sqrt{2\pi}} \exp\left\{-\frac{\left(e_i / \sigma\right)^2}{2}\right\}$$

We now make another assumption that the errors are independent of each other. Then the probability (likelihood) of obtaining the following error sequence is the product of these probabilities.

$$p\left(\text{error}\right) = \prod_{i=1}^{N} p\left(e_i\right)$$

Now, taking the logarithm of the above equation on both sides we have an expression for logarithm of the likelihood.

$$\log\left(\text{likelihood}\right) = \sum_{i=1}^{N} \log\left[p(e_i)\right] = \frac{-N}{2} \log\left(2\pi\right) - \frac{1}{2\sigma^2} \sum_{i=1}^{N} e_i^2$$

Let us examine our motivation for doing that. If we arrange a sequence of numbers in ascending or descending order and take their logarithms in sequence, the logarithms are guaranteed to be in ascending or descending order, as the case may be. We might say that transforming a set of numbers into their logarithms preserves their ranks. Therefore, maximizing the log-likelihood is equivalent to maximizing the likelihood. We shall see in the following discussion that the log-likelihood can be simpler to deal with.

Examining the expression for logarithm of the likelihood, we see that the only variable term is $-\sum_{i=1}^{N} e_i^2$. Note that this is the sum of squared errors multiplied by the negative sign. Thus, maximizing the logarithm of the likelihood is the same as minimizing the sum of squared errors. Therefore, in situations where we make the assumptions as discussed, then the sum of squares multiplied by a negative sign may be used as a proxy for the maximum likelihood.

CHAPTER 3

Factor Models

INTRODUCTION

Factor models are models that are used to explain the risk/return characteristics of assets. It is actually a rather loose term that serves to describe a wide
variety of models. However, all the models share the common characteristic
that they may be viewed as extensions to the CAPM model. The premise of
the CAPM model is that the returns of assets are explicable almost completely by the behavior of the overall market. Each asset is sensitive to the
market in its own characteristic way, and this sensitivity is termed *beta*.

Thus in the CAPM model there is a single explanatory factor and exposure value; namely, the market return and beta. A natural extension to this idea would then be to have multiple explanatory factors and exposure/sensitivity values. For instance, it is possible to construe that the return on a stock depends on the sector of the economy in which it operates, the market capitalization, and a good number of other explanatory factors that can be drawn from the available repertoire of market variables. In this context of multiple explanatory factors, the return of a stock would then be an aggregate of the return contributions of the factors scaled according to the sensitivity/factor exposure. Thus, the return of a stock in a factor model is explained by the return contributions of the various factors.

Depending on the type of the factors used, factor models may be loosely categorized into three main groups: statistical factor models, macroeconomic factor models, and fundamental factor models. The factors in a statistical factor model are what we shall call *eigen* portfolios. They are a set of building-block portfolios with the property that their returns are uncorrelated with each other. Also, the return on any portfolio can be expressed as a linear combination of the returns on the eigen portfolios. However, the eigen portfolios are actually statistical artifacts deduced from data, and interpreting the results is a task that is easier said than done. So, when looking to answer questions from a valuation or a risk control standpoint, one would have to examine the returns closely to answer the question: What is the predominant theme or themes that characterize the eigen portfolio? It is this problem of interpretation that makes the statistical factor models more of a black box and hard to use. Not surprisingly, the preference for practitioners has been models that allow them to specify the factors (macroeconomic or fundamental) allowing for a more intuitive explanation for the factor returns. These models are different from the statistical factor model in that the role of the eigen portfolios is actually assumed by some macroeconomic or fundamental variable that can be observed directly.

The macroeconomic factor models are constructed using historical stock returns and observable macroeconomic variables. An example of proprietary macroeconomic factor models is the Burmeister, Ibbotson, Roll, and Ross (BIRR) model. The factors or attributes in such models typically include short-term bond yield changes, long-term bond yield changes, dollar value versus other currencies, investor confidence, and changes in long-run economic growth. In contrast to the macroeconomic model, the fundamental factor model uses company and industry attributes and market data as raw descriptors to explain the returns. Examples of commercially available models of this type are the BARRA and Wilshire Atlas models. The inputs to these models are typically industry factors comprising the industries in which the firms operate, and other fundamental factors like price/earnings ratio, the price/book ratio, attributes relating to the capital structure of the firm like debt/equity ratios, and the like.

Even though there exists a wide variety of models, it may not be necessary to discuss each of the models on an individual basis. The theoretical underpinning for the models is provided by arbitrage pricing theory (APT). Thus, by treating the factors used as inputs in an abstract way and discussing arbitrage pricing theory, we can cover a lot of ground on the behavior and use of these different models.

ARBITRAGE PRICING THEORY

Arbitrage pricing theory was originally proposed by Stephen A. Ross in 1976. Unlike the preceding introduction, in which APT was presented as an extension of CAPM, the original proposal by Ross is actually embedded in an arbitrage argument and is appropriately reflected in the name of the theory. In this chapter, however, we will avoid an elaborate discussion on the foundations of APT. For that, we direct the reader to the material listed in the references. Instead, we will provide simple definitions and focus on a few applications to familiarize the reader with the concepts and their application.

In the multifactor framework, an asset is fully characterized by its factor exposure/sensitivity profile. The contribution to the overall asset return due to each factor is commensurate with the exposure/sensitivity of the asset to the different factors. The total return is the aggregate of the contributions. Therefore, if APT was to be summed up in one sentence, it would probably be something like this: "Give me the risk factor profile of a security, and I will tell you all about its risk and return characteristics." Let us now describe some terminology and notation surrounding APT.

We will first start with risk factor exposures. Keeping with the idea of APT being an extension of the CAPM model, let us denote the factor exposures as $\left(\beta_1, \beta_2, \beta_3, \ldots, \beta_k\right)$. If $\left(r_1, r_2, r_3, \ldots, r_k\right)$ denote the return contributions of each factor, then the return on the stock is given as

$$r = \beta_1 r_1 + \beta_2 r_2 + \beta_3 r_3 + \ldots + \beta_k r_k + r_e \tag{3.1}$$

where r_e is the idiosyncratic return or specific return on the stock that is not explicable by the factors in the model. One of the key assumptions of APT is that the specific return for a given stock is uncorrelated with both the factor returns and the specific returns of any other stock.

Let us now focus on the evaluation of risk. The risk in a stock is measured as the variance of the return. The variance of return may in some ways be likened to the range of possible values that the return can assume. A small variance is indicative of a narrow range and therefore lower risk, whereas a large variance or wide range is indicative of higher uncertainty in the returns and therefore greater risk. This approach to measuring risk as the second moment of the return distributions was originally proposed by Markowitz, in the context of portfolio optimization. The Markowitz approach to portfolio design is also sometimes referred to as mean-variance optimization and was awarded the Nobel Prize in economics. Today it has become common practice to use the variance of the return as a measure of risk. We will also keep with this practice and illustrate how risk/variance of return is calculated in the APT framework. We do this by way of an example. Let us consider an APT model with two factors.

The returns on the stock in the two factor model case is given as

$$r = \beta_1 r_1 + \beta_2 r_2 + r_e \tag{3.2}$$

The risk is then measured as the variance of this return. To evaluate it, let us first expand the squared return of the stock using the algebraic identity

$$(a + b + c)^2 = a^2 + b^2 + 2ab + 2ac + 2bc + c^2 \tag{3.3}$$

We then have

$$r^2 = \beta_1^2 r_1^2 + \beta_2^2 r_2^2 + 2\beta_1\beta_2 r_1 r_2 + 2\beta_1 r_1 r_e + 2\beta_2 r_2 r_e + r_e^2 \tag{3.4}$$

Applying expectations on both sides and using the formulas in the appendix in the first chapter, we have

$$\text{var}(r) = \beta_1^2 \, \text{var}(r_1) + \beta_2^2 \, \text{var}(r_2) + 2\beta_1\beta_2 \, \text{cov}(r_1, r_2) + \text{var}(r_e) \tag{3.5}$$

Note that since r_e is uncorrelated with both r_1 and r_2, the terms with their products do not feature on the value for the variance. Also, Equation 3.5 can be written in matrix form as follows:

$$\text{var}(r) = \begin{bmatrix} \beta_1 & \beta_2 \end{bmatrix} \begin{bmatrix} \text{var}(r_1) & \text{cov}(r_1, r_2) \\ \text{cov}(r_1, r_2) & \text{var}(r_2) \end{bmatrix} \begin{bmatrix} \beta_1 \\ \beta_2 \end{bmatrix} + \text{var}(r_e) \tag{3.6}$$

Notice the structure of the equation. We have the factor exposure profile and its transpose on either side of a square matrix. This square matrix is structured such that it has the variance of the factor returns on its diagonal and the covariance as the off-diagonal elements. It is also commonly referred to as the covariance matrix of factor returns and plays a central role in the calculation of the risk of the security. We can simplify the notation for risk even further:

$$\text{var}(r) = eVe^T + \text{var}(r_e) \tag{3.7}$$

where V is the covariance matrix and e is the factor exposure vector. Also note from Equation 3.7 that the variance of the return is expressed as a simple sum of two terms. The first term is the variance due to the common factors, and the second term is the idiosyncratic/specific variance. Also, given that the standard deviation is the square root of variance, Equation 3.7 may also be written as

$$\sigma^2_{\text{ret}} = \sigma^2_{\text{cf}} + \sigma^2_{\text{specific}} \tag{3.8}$$

One can easily remember the formula by drawing parallels between this and the Pythagorean theorem from high school geometry. The standard deviations may be represented as the sides of a right-angled triangle as shown in Figure 3.1. In practice, it turns out that the specific variance is the smaller component of the total variance, and a significant portion of the total variance is explained by the common factor variance. Note that key to the evaluation of the common factor variance is the knowledge of the covariance matrix of factor returns.

So, how is the covariance matrix calculated in practice? If we have a sample of past historic factor returns, then it is a simple matter of using the formulas in the appendix of the first chapter to evaluate each of the entries of the covariance matrix. The question therefore now becomes, how do we get a sample of past historic factor returns? To do this, we first write out the linear equations for the return of each stock with known stock returns, treating the factor returns as unknown variables. Next, we solve this system of equations to obtain an estimate of the factor and specific returns. We now have the past factor returns that may be used to estimate the covariance matrix.

In other words, the covariance matrix can be deduced from the factor returns. The converse of this statement is also true. Knowledge of the

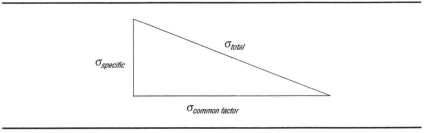

FIGURE 3.1 The Risk Diagram.

covariance matrix with the factor exposures and specific variances is sufficient for us to deduce the vector of expected factor returns. The reader is referred to the book by Grinold and Kahn on how that is done. Consequently, knowledge of the factor covariance matrix and the specific variances is sufficient in order to specify an APT model completely. With that said, let us formally list the parameters that are typically provided in the specification of a factor model. They are as follows:

- *Factor Exposure Matrix.* This is the matrix of exposure/sensitivity factors. If there are N stocks in our universe and k factors in the model, we can construct a $N \times k$ matrix with the exposures for each stock in a row. Let us denote this matrix as X.
- *Factor Covariance Matrix.* This is denoted as V.
- *Specific Variance Matrix.* This is the specific variance for each of the N stocks assembled in an $N \times N$ matrix with the specific variances on the diagonal. Because the specific variances are assumed to be uncorrelated, the nondiagonal elements are zero. This matrix is denoted as Δ.

Of the three parameters, the factor covariance matrix is by far the most interesting. We will therefore discuss some of the properties of the covariance matrix in its own section.

THE COVARIANCE MATRIX

The factor covariance matrix plays a key role in the determination of the risk. It is in fact a square matrix. In a model with k factors, the dimensions of the covariance matrix is $k \times k$. The diagonal elements form the variance of the individual factors, and the nondiagonal elements are the covariances and may have nonzero values. A nonzero covariance implies that the returns of two explanatory factors share some correlation. For example, consider the situation where market capitalization and the leverage of the firm are used as explanatory variables. It is not uncommon within an industry to find that the small cap names have a high amount of leverage. If we assume that the small cap names outperformed the overall market, then we can expect to see a nonzero correlation between the returns attributed to the leverage and capitalization factors. Hence, it is possible to have nonzero entries in the off-diagonal elements of the covariance matrix.

The covariance matrix is also symmetric. This is self-evident because the (i,j)th element and the (j,i)th element contain the entry for the covariance between the ith factor and the jth factor and are therefore the same. Additionally, the covariance matrix is also positive definite. This means that the matrix has a square root; that is, $V = B^2$ for some B, where V, B are matrices.

Consider the situation where we are required to evaluate the covariance between the returns of securities A and B. Let e_A and e_B be the factor exposure vectors for the two stocks. Adapting the formula for variance previously discussed, we have the covariance as

$$\text{cov}(r_A, r_B) = e_A V e_B^T \qquad (3.9)$$

We can therefore calculate the covariance between all the securities in our universe and make them entries in a covariance matrix. This matrix would come in handy to evaluate correlations between securities. Note that if the total universe of securities is about 5000 stocks, then the covariance matrix for the list is a square matrix with 25 million entries. Calculating the variance and covariance of each stock pair individually by sampling past data can be a tedious endeavor. Armed with the factor exposure vectors and the factor covariance matrix, the covariance and correlations between securities may be calculated readily. Thus, the use of the factor covariance matrix reduces the complexity of evaluating the correlations between securities in a dramatic way. Even so, the full and complete covariance matrix for all the stocks in the universe is given by

$$\text{CovMatrix} = X V X^T \qquad (3.10)$$

It is also prudent to be aware of certain potential issues when working with the factor covariance matrix. For example, it is not uncommon in investment circles to hear someone say, "But you don't want to be mining the covariance matrix!" Let us examine what they mean by that. *Mining* here refers to data mining, albeit with a negative connotation. The word is used synonymously with *bias*, indicating that since the covariance matrix is deduced from historical data, the values are a reflection of the past and may not hold going forward. While the empirical observation has been that the covariance matrices are relatively stable, it is still subject to the fact that the values used in the covariance matrix may not be exact, and it may be useful to do some sensitivity analysis on applications where we use the covariance matrix. It is probably worthwhile to also bear in mind that along with the covariance matrix, the specific variance is also backward looking and is subject to the "mining syndrome."

Another issue that is commonly cited with regard to the covariance matrix and its use is the underlying assumption of the Gaussian distribution for the computed variance. The so-called fat tails that are ubiquitous in the variance of returns in financial time series are not accounted for by the model.

Nevertheless, in the absence of any information whatsoever, the covariance matrix serves as a critical piece of information to assess correlations between securities and for use in factor models. Careful use of the covariance matrix can help keep the reconciliation process between the risk and return of a large universe of securities tractable.

Example

Factor exposure for stock A in two-factor model = (0.5, 0.75)

The specific variance on stock A = .0123

The factor covariance matrix for the two-factor model is = $\begin{bmatrix} .0625 & .0225 \\ .0225 & .1024 \end{bmatrix}$

The variance of return for the stock

$$A = \begin{bmatrix} 0.5 & 0.75 \end{bmatrix} \begin{bmatrix} .0625 & .0225 \\ .0225 & .1024 \end{bmatrix} \begin{bmatrix} 0.5 \\ 0.75 \end{bmatrix} + .0123$$

$$= .0901 + .0123$$

$$= .1024$$

The square root of the variance is the standard deviation = .32, or 32%. Thus, stock A has a volatility value of 32%.

Factor exposures for stock B in the two-factor model = (0.75, 0.5)

Covariance between stocks

$$A \text{ and } B = \begin{bmatrix} 0.5 & 0.75 \end{bmatrix} \begin{bmatrix} .0625 & .0225 \\ 0.225 & .1024 \end{bmatrix} \begin{bmatrix} 0.75 \\ 0.5 \end{bmatrix} = 0.0801$$

APPLICATION: CALCULATING THE RISK ON A PORTFOLIO

In the earlier sections we discussed how the APT model may be used to calculate the risk on a particular asset. Now we will focus on assessing the risk of an entire portfolio. Just as with a single security, the risk can be expressed as a sum of two components; namely, common factor risk and specific risk. We will adopt the approach in which we reason out the formulas for each of these components, leading in turn to the expression for the risk in a portfolio.

Let us start with the common factor variance for a security, which can be computed if we know the factor exposures for the security and the factor covariance matrix. The logic to evaluate the common factor variance for the

---

TALKING POINTS

Bear in mind that the APT model is a linear model; that is, the return is a linear combination of factor returns. Is that a limitation of the model? Some would argue that linearity in returns is probably valid only in a fixed range of values for the factor exposures. As the values stretch more and more to the extremes, linearity leads to progressively poor predictions of asset returns. This is akin to quite a few phenomena encountered in the physical sciences where linear relationships are valid only in a certain operating range.

With that said, if you happen to find yourself in a finance conference, in the middle of a discussion on APT at cocktail hour, here is something to try out. Look to a distance, put a finger to your cheek and proclaim wistfully, "I wonder what the consequences are of neglecting the potentially inherent nonlinearities in the modeling process. . . ."

In all likelihood, this will cause a whole lot of other people to also wonder with you. If, however, someone were to probe further and ask you to elaborate on your musings, you could always pretend to recognize someone at a distance, smile politely, and excuse yourself, saying that you need to mingle.

---

portfolio is also along the same lines. If we are able to evaluate the net factor exposure for the portfolio, then we can treat it as a single security and evaluate the common factor variance using the formula discussed in the previous section. Let us therefore concentrate our efforts on the evaluation of the factor exposure for the portfolio. The factor exposure of the portfolio is simply the weighted sum of the factor exposures of all the securities in it. The weight to be used for the exposure of each security is determined by the weight of the security in the portfolio.

Let us consider a portfolio composed of two securities, A and B, with exposure vectors given by e_A and e_B. Let the weights of the two securities in the portfolio be h_A and h_B, respectively. The exposure vector of the portfolio is given as

$$e_p = h_A e_A + h_B e_B \tag{3.11}$$

Assuming a two-factor model and writing out the formula in matrix form, we have

$$e_p = \begin{bmatrix} h_A & h_B \end{bmatrix} \begin{bmatrix} \beta_{A,1} & \beta_{A,2} \\ \beta_{B,1} & \beta_{B,2} \end{bmatrix} \tag{3.12}$$

or

$$e_p = hX \tag{3.13}$$

That is, the exposure of a portfolio is given by the matrix product of the holdings vector and the exposure matrix. Using the value in Equation 3.13 for the factor exposure of the portfolio, the common factor variance is given by substituting the calculated exposure value:

$$\sigma_{cf}^2 = e_p V e_p^T \tag{3.14}$$

Performing the substitutions and applying the matrix identity on the transpose of a matrix product, we have

$$\sigma_{cf}^2 = hXVX^T h^T \tag{3.15}$$

Let us now tackle the specific risk component. The specific risk is calculated as the variance of the specific return. Now, the specific return on the portfolio is the sum of the specific returns of the assets in the portfolio weighted by the share of the security in the portfolio holdings. Also, note that by model assumptions the specific returns of the securities are uncorrelated with each other. If the returns are uncorrelated with each other, then the overall variance is a weighted sum of the individual specific variances. In the preceding two-security example, the specific variance is given as

$$\sigma_{\text{specific}}^2 = h_1^2 \, \text{var}\!\left(r_{e,A}\right) + h_2^2 \, \text{var}\!\left(r_{e,B}\right) \tag{3.16}$$

Writing this out in matrix form, we have

$$\sigma_{\text{specific}}^2 = \begin{bmatrix} h_1 & h_2 \end{bmatrix} \begin{bmatrix} \text{var}\!\left(r_{e,A}\right) & 0 \\ 0 & \text{var}\!\left(r_{e,B}\right) \end{bmatrix} \begin{bmatrix} h_1 \\ h_2 \end{bmatrix} \tag{3.17}$$

or

$$\sigma_{\text{specific}}^2 = h \Delta h^T \tag{3.18}$$

Adding it all together we are now able to put down an expression for the total risk in a portfolio based on the portfolio holdings and the parameters of the APT model. The risk/portfolio variance is therefore given as

$$\sigma^2_{\text{portfolio}} = \sigma^2_{cf} + \sigma^2_{\text{specific}} \tag{3.19}$$

$$= hXVX^T h^T + h\Delta h^T$$

The formula to evaluate the variance may be easily adapted to evaluate the covariance between two portfolios. We will leave it to the reader to reason out that the covariance between two portfolios Y and Z is given by

$$\text{cov}(r_Y, r_Z) = h_Y XVX^T h_Z^T + h_Y \Delta h_Z^T \tag{3.20}$$

In any case, the formula for variance in Equation 3.20 can be used to calculate the risk in a portfolio.

Assuming normality, a two-standard-deviation movement on either side of the daily mark to market should be able to catch the price movement for the next day, 95 percent of the time. Yet in practice that may not turn out to be the case. Let us therefore examine the points of failure of the model. We start by listing the inputs to the risk calculation and then examine the different scenarios. The key inputs are the factor exposures and the covariance matrix.

When a big news event occurs with respect to a particular stock, the factor exposures that we use in the model for that stock are no longer valid. The market now trades on the expectation that the factor exposures after the news event are likely to be a lot different. The covariance structure between the factors is still intact. In any case, since the factor exposure input to the risk model is no longer valid, the calculation breaks down for that particular stock.

The second scenario is the occurrence of a scenario-altering, huge macroeconomic event, for example, relating to interest rates. The big event typically manifests itself in the form of a liquidity crisis. In these situations, the covariance structure breaks down, leading to the breakdown of the model.

Another explanation for observing price moves of more than two standard deviations of that expected by the Gaussian assumption is attributed to the nonnormal fat-tailed distribution of asset returns observed in practice. This can be somewhat addressed by calibrating the number of standard deviations to use in our assessment of the range of price movement. It is therefore important that users of the multifactor technology also be aware of the potential points of failure in the model.

APPLICATION: CALCULATION OF PORTFOLIO BETA

The topic of this section is more of a misnomer, and it likely to strike the reader as an anomaly. We had earlier stated that the APT is a more advanced version of CAPM. Then, if we have access to the APT model, why would we want to calculate the parameters of a simpler CAPM model? Is that not going back full circle? That would indeed be true. However, if we are looking to hedge our portfolio with the market portfolio, then the hedge ratio that provides the best possible hedge is given by the beta of the portfolio. Therefore, it does make sense to calculate beta. While the title may as well read "Determination of Hedge Ratio," having the word *beta* in the title helps make the association between beta and the hedge ratio explicit.

To see the relationship between beta and the hedge portfolio, consider the linear combination of the two portfolios in the ratio $1{:}\lambda$. The return of the linear combination is given by $r_p - \lambda r_m$, where r_p is the return on the portfolio and r_m is the return on the market. The value of λ that results in the least return variance of the combined portfolio is indeed the best hedge ratio. To evaluate the variance of the return, we will apply the algebraic identity

$$\left(a + b\right)^2 = a^2 + b^2 + 2ab \tag{3.21}$$

to the combined portfolio.

$$\left(r_p - \lambda r_m\right)^2 = r_p^2 + \lambda^2 r_m^2 - 2\lambda r_p r_m \tag{3.22}$$

Applying expectations on both sides and using the formulas in the appendix of Chapter 1, we have

$$\mathrm{var}\left(r_p - \lambda r_m\right) = \mathrm{var}\left(r_p\right) + \lambda^2 \,\mathrm{var}\left(r_m\right) - 2\lambda \,\mathrm{cov}\left(r_p r_m\right) \tag{3.23}$$

To find the value for λ that minimizes the variance, we differentiate with respect to λ and equate the differential to zero. It is easy to then see that

$$\lambda = \frac{\mathrm{cov}\left(r_p, r_m\right)}{\mathrm{var}\left(r_m\right)} \tag{3.24}$$

Equation 3.24 also happens to be the definition of beta, and we therefore conclude that beta is the best hedge ratio. Equation 3.24 is composed of the covariance and the variance terms, which we know how to evaluate in the APT framework. Applying the substitutions, we have

$$\lambda = \frac{e_p V e_m^T + h_p \Delta h_m^T}{e_m V e_m^T + h_m \Delta h_m^T} \tag{3.25}$$

where e_p and e_m are the factor exposures of the portfolio and the market, and h_p and h_m are their respective holdings vectors. We are thus able to evaluate the optimal hedge ratio.

APPLICATION: TRACKING BASKET DESIGN

A tracking basket is a basket of stocks that tracks an index. If the basket is the same as the index, then the prices of both will be the same at all times. However, if the tracking basket is composed of fewer stocks than the index, then there is likely to be tracking error; that is, the returns for the tracking basket are not exactly the same as the returns for the index. The discrepancy in the returns is expressed in terms of tracking error.

Tracking error may be defined as the standard deviation of the difference in the return between the tracking basket and the index. In the definition of tracking error, the mean value of the difference is assumed to be zero. To see this more clearly, consider a long–short portfolio where we are long the index and short the tracking basket. The expectation is that the return on the index and tracking basket is the same. Therefore, a profit made on one leg of the portfolio is likely to be neutralized by an equal loss on the other leg. The expected value of total return on the portfolio is therefore zero. However, while the expected return is zero, it is possible for the actual return value to be a nonzero value. The extent of this variation from zero is captured by the standard deviation of returns of the long–short portfolio and forms a measure of the tracking error.

A natural deduction from the preceding discussion is that the design of a tracking basket involves designing a portfolio such that it minimizes the tracking error. Writing out the equations for the variance of the error in returns, we have

$$\text{Min: } E\left(r_m - r_p\right)^2 = \text{var}\left(r_m\right) + \text{var}\left(r_p\right) - 2\,\text{cov}\left(r_m r_p\right) \qquad (3.26)$$

where r_p is the return on the tracking basket and r_m is the return on the market. Expanding the terms using APT constructs, we have

$$\text{Min: } h_m X V X^T h_m^T + h_m \Delta h_m^T + h_p X V X^T h_p^T + h_p h_p^T - \qquad (3.27)$$
$$- 2\left[h_m X V X^T h_p^T + h_m \Delta h_p\right]$$

Bear in mind that there are some constraints on the values of h_p; that is, some of them are forced to have zero values even though they are part of the index.

Note that in Equation 3.27, the variance of the market portfolio is not at all affected by changing the composition of the tracking basket. The only two terms that are affected when we change the tracking basket composition is the tracking basket variance and the covariance term. Therefore, minimizing the tracking error is equivalent to minimizing the sum of the two terms.

The error variance may also be viewed as a sum of two components; namely, a common factor component and a specific component. Now, if we were to design the tracking basket such that the factor exposures of the basket match the factor exposures of the index exactly (even though their contents may not be identical), then the common factor component goes to zero. We are now left only with the specific components of the variance. Recall from our earlier discussion that the contributions to the total variance from the specific components are a lot less than they would be from the common factor component. Furthermore, if the two portfolios are highly diversified, the expected value of the specific returns on the portfolios is zero. Hence, the tracking error contribution in this case is solely due to the different specific returns in the portfolios. It is now easy to appreciate that a good starting point to the design of tracking baskets will ensure that the factor exposures match as closely as possible. Hence, APT constructs may be used to design tracking baskets.

SENSITIVITY ANALYSIS

In our discussion on the covariance matrix we talked about the mining syndrome, the idea being that the estimation of the covariance matrix is biased to the past and may not hold going forward into the future. This apprehension may be objectively examined by studying the stability of the covariance matrix.

One approach would be to estimate a sequence of covariance matrices and study the variations between two consecutive ones. The extent to which the variations affect the particular situation—say, the evaluation of beta, the measurement of risk, or the design of tracking baskets—may be gauged by perturbing the current covariance matrix with the sequence of observed changes and running the calculations with the perturbed matrix.

This results in a set of values for the estimated parameter. We can then treat the set of values as realizations from a probability distribution and get an idea of the error in our estimates using the current covariance matrix to help us quantify the extent of uncertainty due to the mining syndrome.

SUMMARY

- Factor models are models that are used to explain the risk return characteristics of assets and come in many flavors.
- Even though the details may vary, factor models are firmly based on the principles of arbitrage pricing theory (APT).
- A factor model is considered fully specified by the factor exposures, the factor covariance matrix, and the specific variance matrix.
- A factor model may be used as a framework to estimate many commonplace parameters that may be needed in the course of the investment process.
- Examples of such computations include the estimation of risk on a portfolio, the evaluation of portfolio beta, and computing the contents of a tracking basket.
- The factor covariance matrix is a crucial piece of information that the factor model provides. However, it must be used with care.

FURTHER READING MATERIAL

King, Benjamin F. "Market and Industry Factors in Stock Price Behavior." *Journal of Business* 39, no. 1 (1966): 139–190.

Ross, Stephen A. "The Arbitrage Theory of Capital Asset Pricing." *Journal of Economic Theory* 13 (1976): 341–360.

Jarrow, Robert and Andrew Rudd. "A Comparison of the APT and CAPM: A Note." *Journal of Banking and Finance* 7, no. 3 (1983): 295–303.

Grinold, Richard C. and Ronald N. Kahn, *Active Portfolio Management*, Second Edition. (New York: McGraw-Hill, 1999).

CHAPTER 4

Kalman Filtering

INTRODUCTION

Control theory is a branch of engineering that deals with the control of engineering systems. The engineering systems could be from diverse domains, and the applications include controlling the power output of an automotive engine, stabilizing the rate of rotation of an electric motor, and controlling the "rate of reaction" (or the speed of a chemical process). The control of these systems is exercised by the manipulation of so-called control variables. For example, in the case of controlling the power output of an automotive engine, the control variable could be the amount of fuel injected into the engine. This would control the thrust of the piston and therefore the power output from the engine. Similarly, in the other two examples, the control variables could be the amount of current flowing through the motor coils or the ambient temperature of a chemical process. Thus, the control variables provide a harness that helps us to control the system effectively.

Prior to the proposal of Kalman filtering, the typical approach for system control involved the specification of a fully comprehensive mathematical model describing the system dynamics. The model is usually formulated in the form of a differential equation. This helps to determine in a quantitative manner the effects of the control variables on system dynamics. Control is then effected by manipulating the variables as prescribed by the model.

Along with the preceding approach also came a painful realization of its limitations. The mathematical models may not be 100-percent accurate, as there may be some approximations used in the modeling process. Additionally, the instruments used to measure the system parameters may have some built-in inaccuracies that could result in measurement error. To compound things even further, there may also be some extraneous disturbances to the system that cannot be anticipated and modeled in a deterministic fashion. Hence, the aforementioned methodology becomes increasingly harder to implement as the systems grow in complexity.

It was under these circumstances that the Kalman filter was proposed by R. E. Kalman. He addressed these issues in a direct and practical manner and presented his ideas in a ground-breaking article[1] titled "A New Approach to Linear Filtering and Prediction Problems." The approach caught the attention and imagination of the engineering community, and the ideas found application in multiple domains.

One of the key contributions of Kalman's article is the notion of *system state*," or the current state of the system. It is represented as a vector of the current values of various system parameters. The vector itself is deduced from a set of measurements on the system that is in turn translated into system-state terms. This translation is typically modeled as a linear equation. Thus, the means to make observations and the equation translating the observation into the system state fully characterize the notion of system state.

Having established the notion of system state, Kalman proceeded to cast a dynamical system in terms of system states. A dynamical system in the Kalman-filtering approach is modeled as a sequence of transitions from one system state to another. These transitions are also modeled as linear equations.

Next, he asserted that to monitor the system effectively (for purposes of control) it makes sense to make an assessment of the state that we are currently in and the state that we expect to transition to in the next time step. In other words, we are in a situation where we are constantly predicting the next system state and taking measurements to verify the predictions. The Kalman filter provides a prescription to reconcile this sequence of predictions followed by measurements to arrive at a sequence of optimal estimates for system states. This approach to thinking of systems as a sequence of state transitions was a radical departure from the thinking at the time. It started a revolution of sorts in the field of control theory and marks the beginning of a new era in the field commonly referred to by many as *Modern Control Theory*.

So, how does this fit into our scheme of things? For one, we use the Kalman-filtering technique to filter the noise from the observed spread in the case of risk arbitrage. Describing this in the introduction therefore helps provide the context for its application later in the book.

To help to illustrate the Kalman-filtering ideas and also as a matter of interest, we apply the Kalman-filtering concepts to smooth out a random walk. Now, many practitioners of technical analysis make use of so-called moving averages to smooth out or filter price series. This method of using moving averages may be thought of as an attempt to estimate the sequence of stock prices (states) after filtering out the noise. The common peeve

[1]Kalman, R. E. (1960). "A New Approach to Filtering and Prediction Problems." Transaction of the ASME Journal of Basic Engineering, 82(Series D), 35–45.

The practical nature of the modeling process and solution approach made the Kalman filter immediately applicable to a wide variety of situations. In fact, one of the first applications of the Kalman filter was in the lunar module of Apollo 11, the spacecraft for the first landing on the Moon. Therefore, if anything in the book should qualify as rocket science, this definitely fits the bill. ☺

against the moving averages has always been that they tend to lag when there is a sharp and sudden change in price movement. The Kalman filter can help construct better smoothers. Although we do not delve deeply into the matter, we believe that this approach may very well contain the seeds of reasoning for the observation of the so-called Fibonacci retracements, which is well documented in the area of technical analysis.

THE KALMAN FILTER

Continuing on the theme of the previous section, the Kalman-filtering process can best be described as a three-step process of prediction, observation, and reconciliation or correction. In the prediction step, we predict the next system state based on our knowledge of the current system state. Along with it, we also estimate the error in our prediction. This completes the prediction step.

Next we take a reading of the state of the system after allowing for a fixed amount of time to elapse, the idea being that the system would now have transitioned to the new state. The readings can be translated in system-state terms based on a mathematical model. Similar to the prediction step, we also estimate the error associated with our observation. The observation along with an estimate of the error constitutes the observation step.

We now have two estimates for the states involved: one based on our prediction and the other based on our observation. The natural next step is then to reconcile the two state estimates, taking into account the magnitude of the associated errors. Stating it differently, the predicted estimate is corrected based on the observation. This is therefore called the correction step. This reconciled estimate of the system state from the correction step is the final estimate of the current system state.

The preceding process is then repeated again for the state at the next time instance, making the Kalman filter a recursive prediction–correction method. The preceding steps are also illustrated in the form of a diagram in Figure 4.1.

The reader is probably now curious as to how the correction to the predicted value is effected. Let us discuss that briefly. Note that it is possible to translate the prediction of the next state into a set of expected observations.

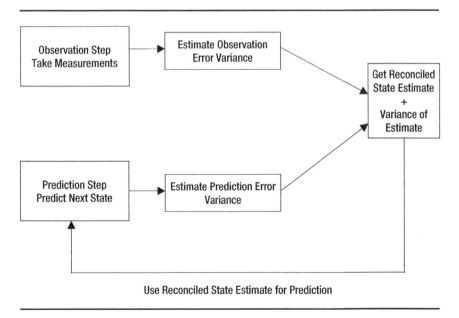

FIGURE 4.1 The Kalman Filtering Process.

Let us call this as the predicted observation. The equation for the corrected state in a Kalman filter is given as

corrected State = predicted state + k (actual observation –
– predicted observation)

The difference between the actual observation and the predicted observation is called the *observation innovation*. Note that a fraction of the observation innovation is added as a correction to the predicted state. The value of this fraction k is known as the Kalman gain. The Kalman-filtering approach provides a prescription on what would be the most appropriate value to use for k. This value is decided such that the corrected state has the least amount of error variance associated with it.

Besides providing the prescription to reconcile the prediction and observation, Kalman also provided definitive proof that the process is indeed optimal in the case where the mathematical models of state and observation are both linear and the errors are drawn from independent Gaussian distributions. We will, of course, not delve into the proofs, but rather try to explain the basic idea by way of illustrations. With that said, we introduce some notation and formally list the steps involved in the Kalman-filtering process.

Let X_t denote the state at time t. Note that the value for the state can also be a vector; that is, the state has a multidimensional representation. The mathematical model used to predict the state at time t in a Kalman filter setting is typically of the form

$$X_t = AX_{t-1} + u_t \tag{4.1}$$

where A is a matrix, X_t and X_{t-1} are the state vectors at time t and $t-1$, respectively, and u_t is the error vector that accounts for the impreciseness of the model. Next we make an observation at time t. Let us call this observation Y_t. The measurements made are a linear combination of the state elements and therefore can be written as

$$Y_t = HX_t + v_t \tag{4.2}$$

In this scenario the values of the matrices A and H are known. Initially we make a prediction of the state at time t, knowing all the state information up to time $t-1$. Let us denote this estimate $\hat{X}_{t|t-1}$. The error is measured as the variance in the case of a single dimensional state and as a covariance matrix in the case of a multidimensional state.

Let us denote it generally as $\hat{P}_{t|t-1}$. Just as in the case of the predicted value, the measurement also has an error variance/covariance matrix associated with it. Let us call that R. We are now ready to formally list the steps in the Kalman-filtering process as follows:

1. Evaluate $\hat{X}_{t|t-1}$ and $\hat{P}_{t|t-1}$ using the state equation.
2. Find the observation Y_t and R by observing the system.
3. Evaluate K_t, also known as the Kalman gain, which will be used to obtain the linear minimum error variance estimate.
4. Evaluate $\hat{X}_{t|t}$ given by $\hat{X}_{t|t-1} + K_t \left(Y_t - H\hat{X}_{t|t-1} \right)$.
5. Finally, evaluate P_t, the error variance/covariance of $\hat{X}_{t|t}$.

These steps are repeated again for the next time step. The formulas for the evaluations at each step are relegated to the appendix at the end of this chapter. Upon examining the equations in the appendix, one can say that they do seem a little cryptic, and the reasoning and rationale behind them is not evident. In the subsequent sections we will illustrate the ideas behind the equations.

THE SCALAR KALMAN FILTER

In this section, we will discuss the estimation of the value of a constant. Let us first examine how to do it in normal course. The typical method would be to take multiple measurements of the value and use the average of the measured values as an estimate of the constant. The reasoning behind the approach is that the measurements could have errors associated with them; that is, some measured values could be greater than the true value of the constant, and others could be lower. By taking an average of the values, we expect the errors to cancel each other out. More precisely, the standard deviation of the error in the average goes down by a square root of n factor, where n is the number of measurements.

The consequence of this method is in fact a well-known statistical concept. By increasing the number of observations of a constant variable and taking averages, we can make the error in our estimate of the constant as small as desired.

However, a caveat to that approach is that we will need to wait until the last of the n measurements have been completed before coming up with an estimate of the constant (which may not be a bad idea at all). The Kalman filter, however, makes an estimate of the value of the constant based on the current available information and updates the estimate as and when more observations are made. Of course, the result after n observations in both cases will be the same.

Note that if the error variances associated with different observations are the same, then a simple average will be fine. However, in the case where the observed values have different levels of accuracy, we would like to assign more weight to the observations with greater accuracy. In such cases, instead of taking a simple average that weights each point uniformly, a weighted average solution would be more appropriate. We will illustrate how to address the weighted average situation using the Kalman filter concepts and thereby hope to provide some insight to the calculation of the Kalman gain.

In the estimation of the constant value, the system state is the one-dimensional constant value itself. Let us say that our current estimate of the constant value is $\hat{x}_i$ with error in the estimate being ε_i, that is,

$$\hat{x}_{i|i} = x + \varepsilon_i \tag{4.3}$$

x is the true value of the constant. Although we do not know what the exact value of ε_i is, we do know that it has a zero mean and known variance given by $\sigma_{\varepsilon,i}^2$. Let us now do the prediction step. Since the value stays a constant, our prediction for the next state is the current value itself. Therefore, we have

$$\hat{x}_{i+1|i} = \hat{x}_i, \operatorname{var}\left(\hat{x}_{i+1|i}\right) = \sigma_{\varepsilon,i}^2 \tag{4.4}$$

Next we make a measurement. Let us call the measurement of the constant value y_i and the error associated with it η_i with zero mean and known variance given as $\sigma_{\eta,i}^2$. Therefore at the end of the measurement step, we have the observation

$$y_i = x + \eta_i, \operatorname{var}\left(y_i\right) = \sigma_{\eta,i}^2 \tag{4.5}$$

We now have a prediction and an observation, and we wish to reconcile the two values. We do this in the reconciliation/correction step where we correct the predicted value based on the observation. Writing out the correction equation, we have

$$\hat{x}_{i+1|i+1} = \hat{x}_{i+1|i} + k\left(y_i - \hat{x}_{i+1|i}\right) \tag{4.6}$$

Note that this can be rewritten as

$$\hat{x}_{i+1|i+1} = \left(1 - k\right)\hat{x}_{i+1|i} + ky_i \tag{4.7}$$

That is, the corrected state estimate is a weighted average of the two state estimates, with k, the Kalman gain, being the weight. The choice for the

Kalman gain must be such that the error variance of the final estimated state is minimized. Writing out the variance for the final state estimate we have

$$\text{var}\left(\hat{x}_{i+1|i+1}\right) = \left(1 - k\right)^2 \text{var}\left(\hat{x}_{i+1|i}\right) + k^2 \text{var}\left(y_i\right) = \left(1 - k\right)^2 \sigma_{\varepsilon,i}^2 + k^2 \sigma_{\eta,i}^2 \quad (4.8)$$

The task is now to find the value of k that minimizes the variance. Instead of doing the derivation mathematically, we will arrive at the value of k by analogy to some high school circuit theory. Consider the parallel circuit as shown in Figure 4.2.

The fraction of current flowing into each arm of the circuit k and $1 - k$ is shown in Equation 4.10. According to Ohm's law, the current flow chooses the path of least resistance, and the flow on each arm is inversely proportional to the resistance of that arm. According to Kirchoff's law, the sum of the current flowing through each arm of the circuit must be equal to the total current flow I. Also, the flow of current is such that minimum energy is expended in the process. The energy of the circuit is given as

$$E = I^2 \left[\left(1 - k\right)^2 R_\varepsilon + k^2 R_\eta\right] \quad (4.9)$$

Equating $R_\varepsilon = \sigma_\varepsilon^2$ and $R_\eta = \sigma_\eta^2$, it is now easy to see the similarity between the two situations. The fraction of current and the Kalman gain is given as

$$k = \frac{\sigma_\varepsilon^2}{\sigma_\eta^2 + \sigma_\varepsilon^2} \quad (4.10)$$

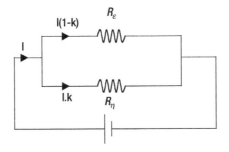

FIGURE 4.2 A Parallel Circuit.

The effective resistance of the circuit or the equivalent variance of the combination is given as

$$R = \text{var}\left(\hat{x}_{i+1|i+1}\right) = \frac{R_\varepsilon R_\eta}{R_\varepsilon + R_\eta} = \frac{\sigma_\varepsilon^2 \sigma_\eta^2}{\sigma_\varepsilon^2 + \sigma_\eta^2} \qquad (4.11)$$

Having determined the value of k, we can now compute the corrected state and the variance of the corrected state. The process is now repeated again for the next measurement until we reach the last of the planned n measurements. The final outcome of taking a weighted average after making all the measurements will work out to be the same value calculated using the Kalman procedure.

FILTERING THE RANDOM WALK

Let us now discuss the application of the Kalman filter to the random walk. From Chapter 2, on time series, we know that a random walk series is a simple sum of white noise realizations up to the current time. In other words, the next point in the random walk series is evaluated by adding to the current point a random drawing from a Gaussian distribution. Also note that this has relevance to stock prices, as the logarithm of stock prices is typically modeled as a random walk.

Now suppose we are assigned the task of watching the random walk. The outcome of the watching exercise is to come up with the random walk series. In stock price terms, the watching exercise translates to coming up with a time series of stock prices. To do that, we observe the prices at regular time intervals and record them. The resulting sequence of values constitutes a random walk, and our mission is accomplished. Note that the last traded price at each instance is known without error, and it is therefore possible to observe the series without error. And if there is no error in the observation, then the Kalman filter model does not apply. So why do we even attempt such an exercise?

We address this matter in the following discussion. Broadly speaking, the price at any given time instance may be construed as the price at which the supply meets demand. Let us call this the equilibrium price. Let us now frame the aim of the watching exercise as generating the sequence of equilibrium prices over consecutive time intervals. In this context, the periodic measurement approach amounts to using the observed price at a specific time as the equilibrium price for the time interval. It is now easy to make the case that the prices at the end of regular chunks of time are indeed approximations of the equilibrium price for the time chunk, and the notion of observation error begins to make sense. It is therefore definitely reasonable to apply Kalman-filtering ideas to stock price series with the logarithm of prices modeled as a random walk.

Summarizing the discussions so far, we have assigned ourselves the task of watching a random walk and making observations at regular time intervals. Each of the observations has a measure of error associated with it. The purpose of the exercise is to come up with a plausible set of system states.

Keeping with the notational conventions already established, let us denote the sequence of observations starting from time $t = 0$, the beginning of our watching exercise as y_t, and the true states as x_t. The observation equation may be written $y_t = x_t + e_t$; that is, the observation is the true state plus some error. Now, according to the definition of the random walk, we also have $x_t = x_{t-1} + \varepsilon_t$ (the current state is the previous state plus an innovation). Writing this as a sequence of predictions and observations, we have

$$y_0 = x_0 + e_0 \qquad \text{(observation)}$$
$$x_1 = x_0 + \varepsilon_1 \qquad \text{(prediction)}$$
$$y_1 = x_1 + e_1 \qquad \text{(observation)}$$
$$x_2 = x_1 + \varepsilon_2 \qquad \text{(prediction)}$$
$$y_2 = x_2 + e_2 \qquad \text{(observation)}$$
$$\dots$$

Writing the equations in matrix form, we have

$$\begin{bmatrix} y_0 \\ 0 \\ y_1 \\ 0 \\ y_2 \end{bmatrix} = \begin{bmatrix} 1 & 0 & 0 \\ -1 & 1 & 0 \\ 0 & 1 & 0 \\ 0 & -1 & 1 \\ 0 & 0 & 1 \end{bmatrix} \begin{bmatrix} x_0 \\ x_1 \\ x_2 \end{bmatrix} + \begin{bmatrix} e_0 \\ -\varepsilon_1 \\ e_1 \\ -\varepsilon_2 \\ e_2 \end{bmatrix}$$

For notational convenience let us denote the system of equations as

$$Y_2 = H_2 X_2 + \eta_2$$

The 2 in the subscript is the index of the state and is indicative of the number of state estimates used in forming the equations. The above is a set of five equations with three unknown values x_0, x_1, x_2. Given that there are more equations than unknowns, the system is also referred to as an overdetermined set. If the errors at each stage are drawn from identical, independent normal distributions, then the typical solution to the overdetermined set is obtained by applying the least squares method:

$$X_2 = \left(H_2^T H_2\right)^{-1} H_2^T Y_2 \qquad (4.12)$$

That is, we multiply both sides by the transpose of H_2, to get a system of three equations with three unknowns and then solve the system of equations. This would be our solution method in the normal course.

Now let us move on to the next observation y_3. Upon obtaining the new data point, the estimate of our state is determined by the solution of the equation

$$Y_3 = H_3 X_3 + \eta_3$$

a system of seven equations with four unknown variables. We could then use the typical approach to solve the overdetermined equations and obtain an estimate for the value of x_3. Note, however, that as the number of observations increases, the size of the matrices grows, and the computational costs could potentially go up. It is here that the Kalman-filtering algorithm comes to our rescue. The results from the previous computations are used in an iterative fashion to estimate the value of the next state. The value of x_2 and its variance as calculated in the previous step is used in the evaluation of the state x_3, thereby keeping the computational cost of evaluating the next step the same regardless of how far down the time scale we are.

Regardless, the end result of the state estimate in the Kalman-filtering case is the same as solving the set of equations using the least squares approach. Note that we have made an important assumption in the process; that is, the state variance at each time step is equal to the observation variance. (This is in addition to the assumption of independence of the error distributions.) Thus, with the preceding assumptions, the Kalman filter boils down to a least squares solution of equations. The twist is that the solution is calculated in a recursive fashion. This version of the Kalman filter is therefore known as the *recursive* least squares method.

The assumption of identical and independent error distributions manifests itself in the covariance matrix of the errors. The independence also implies that the errors are not correlated. Therefore, the off-diagonal elements in the covariance matrix are all zero. The diagonal elements in the covariance matrix are the variances of the error terms. If they are drawn from identical distributions, then the variances should be the same. Therefore, the covariance matrix in this case may be represented as the identity matrix multiplied by a constant.

Let us now turn our attention back to the solution of the preceding model. It turns out that the estimated state at a given time for that set of equations can be represented as a weighted linear combination of the observations. Additionally, the weights are actually ratios of Fibonacci numbers. The Fibonacci sequence of numbers is constructed starting from two seed numbers, $F_0 = 0$ and $F_1 = 1$. The next number in the series is generated by adding the last two numbers in the series, $F_n = F_{n-1} + F_{n-2}$. Applying the formula in an iterative fashion, we obtain the Fibonacci sequence as follows:

$$0, 1, 1, 2, 3, 5, 8, 13, 21, 34, \ldots.$$

There are a variety of situations in which the Fibonacci numbers appear. Some sources of information on Fibonacci numbers are listed in the reference section. In any case, the solution to our problem, that is, the estimate of state x_2, is given as

$$x_2 = \frac{5}{8}y_2 + \frac{2}{8}y_1 + \frac{1}{8}y_0$$

Similarly, x_3 is given as

$$x_3 = \frac{13}{21}y_3 + \frac{5}{21}y_2 + \frac{2}{21}y_1 + \frac{1}{21}y_0$$

In general, if we are to estimate x_T, then

$$x_T = w_0 y_T + w_1 y_{T-1} + w_2 y_{T-2} + \ldots. \tag{4.13}$$

where

$$w_0, w_1, w_2, \ldots, w_T \Big) = \left(\frac{F_{2(T+1)-1}}{F_{2(T+1)}}, \frac{F_{2(T+1)-3}}{F_{2(T+1)}}, \frac{F_{2(T+1)-5}}{F_{2(T+1)}}, \ldots, \frac{F_1}{F_{2(T+1)}} \right) \tag{4.14}$$

Note that the first weight is the ratio of two consecutive Fibonacci numbers. The ratio $\dfrac{F_{2(T+1)}}{F_{2(T+1)-1}}$ approaches the value g. The value g is famously known as the golden mean ratio. It is given by the formula $g = \left(1 + \sqrt{5}\right) / 2$ and has an approximate value of 1.618. The first weight in the observation is actually the reciprocal of the ratio $\frac{1}{g} \approx 0.618$. The subsequent weights are $\frac{1}{g^3}$, $\frac{1}{g^5}$, ... and so on. To see that the second ratio is $\frac{1}{g^3}$, consider the following:

$$\frac{F_{2(T+1)-3}}{F_{2(T+1)}} = \frac{F_{2(T+1)-3}}{F_{2(T+1)-2}} \frac{F_{2(T+1)-2}}{F_{2(T+1)-1}} \frac{F_{2(T+1)-1}}{F_{2(T+1)}} \approx \frac{1}{g^3} \tag{4.15}$$

We will once again draw attention to the fact that the solution presented in Equation 4.15 stays valid only when the state variance is equal to the observation variance. In other situations, we need to obtain an estimate of the state and observation variance at each time step. We will therefore conclude this section with a brief discussion on the estimation of the state and observation variances.

In general random walk terms, the state variance can be estimated as the variance of the innovations. Modeling the stock price series as a random walk, the innovations correspond to the period returns of the price series. The state variance in this case is therefore the variance of the period returns. This calculation is rather commonplace in financial circles and is often referred to as *historic volatility*. The observation variance is, however, a tricky issue. Let us assume that in addition to the closing price in a time interval, we also observe the high and low stock prices within the interval. The variance of the error in the observation must be the volatility of the stock price in the time period. This volatility is characterized by high and low values. Several methods to estimate the volatility based on the high–low prices exist, and the references are provided in the reference section. One may use any one of the methods described in the papers in the appendix to estimate the observation variance. Once the state and observation variances are known, we are ready to apply the Kalman-filtering approach.

APPLICATION: EXAMPLE WITH THE STANDARD & POOR INDEX

Is it conceivable that the observation and innovation variance will be the same? Why not? After all, they are both representative of the volatility of the same underlying random walk. Let us therefore see how we fare in practice. We apply the random walk-filtering process with all its assumptions on the Standard & Poor (S&P) index. We use the closing prices of the S&P index depository receipt (spidr) with ticker SPY in our example. As discussed in the section *Filtering the Random Walk*, we use Equation 4.13 to determine the state of the process at a given time. The weights in Equation 4.15 are determined using Fibonacci numbers. Note that if we decide to use $T + 1$ observations in the state estimation process, the weight of the last data point according to Equation 4.14 is given by $\dfrac{1}{F_{2(T+1)}}$. This is the fraction of the oldest data point used in the estimate. It turns out that this value approaches zero rather quickly, and its contribution to the value of the state becomes insignificant as T increases. In order to demonstrate the point, we constructed a plot of the reciprocals of the Fibonacci series in Figure 4.3.

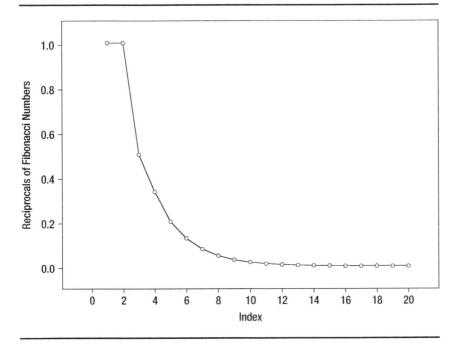

FIGURE 4.3   Reciprocals of Fibonacci Numbers.

Therefore, numerically speaking, it may be sufficient to use, say, the last 10 observations in the state estimation process. Table 4.1 lists the weightings to use for the 10 observations.

With the available weights and the observations, the computation process becomes a simple calculation of the weighted average of the observed values, resulting in a unique sequence of states. This set of states is optimal under the assumptions discussed.

Although this is all nice, note that the typical user of moving averages probably works with them over multiple time periods. The time periods are used to modify the coarseness of the approximation, and it may be argued that looking at moving averages calculated over multiple time frames gives

TABLE 4.1   Reciprocals of Fibonacci Numbers.

1	2	3	4	5	6	7	8	9	10
0.6180	0.2360	0.0901	0.0344	0.0131	0.0050	0.0019	0.0007	0.0002	0.0001

the technical analyst additional information. The question before us now is, therefore, how can we fine-tune the coarseness of the approximations using the Kalman filter?

To achieve varying levels of coarseness using the Kalman filter, we make use of an important property that relates to the sampling of a random walk sequence; that is, the random walk sequence sampled at any frequency results in a random walk sequence. To see why that is, consider a random walk sequence with observations at times 1, 2, 3, and so on. By definition, the observation at time 1 plus a value drawn from a normal distribution gives the observation at time 2, and so on. Now let us sample the random walk at half of the original observation frequency. This results in a new sequence with the values for the times 1, 3, 5, and so on. Note that the value at time 3 is given by the value at time 1 plus a drawing from a normal distribution to get it to time 2, and then again by adding another drawing from a normal distribution to get it to time 3. Thus, the transition from time 1 to time 3 is effected by summing two random drawings from independent normal distributions and, in turn, adding it to the value at time 1. But the sum of

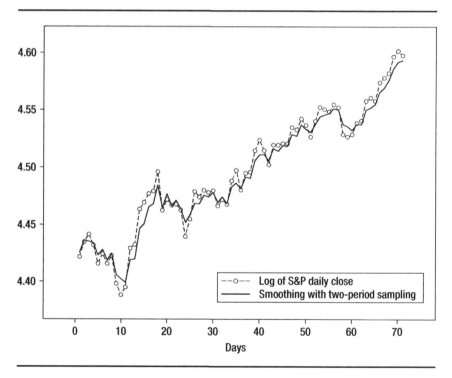

FIGURE 4.4   Kalman Smoothing of Random Walk.

two independent normal random variables may itself be treated as a drawing from a normal distribution with an adjustment to the variance of the distribution. Therefore, the transition from time 1 to time 3 is also effected by adding the value at time = 1 to a drawing from a normal distribution. This therefore fits the definition of a random walk sequence. We only need to apply this idea in an iterative fashion to see that the random walk sequence sampled at any frequency results in a random walk.

Armed with this information, we can conclude that the Kalman smoothing approach may be applied to the random walk sequence sampled at multiple frequencies to achieve varying degrees of coarseness. In our example, we calculate the state values by sampling the random walk at half the frequency of the available data. Suppose we need to calculate the value of the state at time $t = 22$. We use the observations $y_{22}, y_{20}, y_{18}, \ldots$. Similarly, to estimate the state value at time $t = 23$, we use the observation values $y_{23}, y_{21}, y_{19}, \ldots$. The resulting smoothing on the logarithm of the S&P prices is shown in Figure 4.4.

SUMMARY

- The Kalman filter is an optimal state estimation process applied to a dynamic system that involves random perturbations.
- Inherent in any discussion on the Kalman filter are the notions of state and observation.
- Kalman filtering may be summarized as a three-step process comprising prediction, observation, and correction, or reconciliation of the prediction with the observation.
- The simplest case of the Kalman filter reduces to finding the average of n numbers.
- The recursive least squares method is also a special case of the Kalman filter that may be applied to filtering random walks.
- When the state and observation variances are the same, that is, the signal-to-noise ratio is unity, then the estimation of the Kalman states for a random walk boils down to a weighted average of the observations, with the weights formed by ratios of Fibonacci numbers.
- The degree of smoothness to be achieved in a random walk can be controlled by varying the sampling rate of the random walk sequence.

FURTHER READING MATERIAL

Kalman Filter

Maybeck, Peter S. *Stochastic Model, Estimation and Control.* (San Diego, California: Academic Press, 1979).

Harvey, A. C. *Forecasting, Structural Time Series Model and the Kalman Filter.* (Cambridge, UK. Cambridge University Press, 1991).

Variance Calculation

Ismail, Malik Magdon and Amir Atiya. "A Maximum Likelihood Approach to Variance Estimation for a Brownian Motion Using the High Low and Close." *Quantitative Finance* (forthcoming).

Rogers, L. and S. Satchell. "Estimating Variance from High Low and Closing Prices." *Annals of Applied Probability* 1, no. 4 (1991): 504–512.

Rogers, L., S. Satchell and Y. Yoon. "Estimating the Volatility of Stock Prices: A Comparison of Methods That Use High and Low Prices." *Applied Financial Economics* 4 (1994): 241–247.

Fibonacci Series

Huntley, H. E. *The Divine Proportion: A Study in Mathematical Beauty.* (New York: Dover Publications, 1970).

Fischer, Robert. *Fibonacci Applications and Strategies for Traders.* (New York: John Wiley & Sons, Inc., 1993).

APPENDIX

We describe the formulas for the Kalman filtering steps here. The notation we use is the same as that discussed in the section on the Kalman filter.

1. Evaluate $\hat{X}_{t|t-1}$ and $\hat{P}_{t|t-1}$ using the state equation.

$$\hat{X}_{t|t-1} = A\hat{X}_{t-1|t-1}$$
$$\hat{P}_{t|t-1} = A\hat{P}_{t-1|t-1}A^T$$

2. Find the observation Y_t and R by observing the system. Note that we have the matrix H defined as follows:

$$Y_t = HX_t + v_t$$

3. Compute the Kalman gain K_t.

$$K_t = \hat{P}_t H^T \left(H\hat{P}_t H^T + R \right)^{-1}$$

4. Evaluate $\hat{X}_{t|t}$ given by $\hat{X}_{t|t-1} + K_t \left(Y_t - H\hat{X}_{t|t-1} \right)$.

5. Evaluate $\hat{P}_{t|t}$.

$$\hat{P}_{t|t} = \left(1 - KH\right)\hat{P}_{t|t-1}\left(1 - KH\right)^T + KRK^T$$

Statistical Arbitrage Pairs

CHAPTER 5

Overview

HISTORY

The first practice of statistical pairs trading is attributed to Wall Street quant Nunzio Tartaglia, who was at Morgan Stanley in the mid 1980s. At the time, he assembled a group of mathematicians, physicists, and computer scientists. Their mission was to develop quantitative arbitrage strategies using state-of-the-art statistical techniques. The strategies developed by the group were automated to the point where they could generate trades in a mechanical fashion and, if needed, execute them seamlessly through automated trading systems. At that time, trading systems of this kind were considered the cutting edge of technology.

One of the techniques they used for trading involved trading securities in pairs. The process involved identifying pairs of securities whose prices tended to move together. Whenever an anomaly in the relationship was noticed, the pair would be traded with the idea that the anomaly would correct itself. This came to be known on the street as "pairs trading." Tartaglia and his group employed pairs trading with great success in 1987. The group, however, disbanded in 1989. Members of the group found themselves in various other trading firms, and knowledge of the idea of pairs trading gradually spread. Pairs trading has since increased in popularity and has become a common trading strategy used by hedge funds and institutional investors.

MOTIVATION

Let us now explain the idea behind pairs trading. The general theme for investing in the marketplace from a valuation point of view is to sell overvalued securities and buy the undervalued ones. However, it is possible to determine that a security is overvalued or undervalued only if we also know the true value of the security in absolute terms. But, this is very hard to do. Pairs trading attempts to resolve this using the idea of relative pricing; that is, if two securities have similar characteristics, then the prices of both securities must be more or less the same. Note that the specific price of the security is not of importance. The price may be wrong. It is only important that the prices of the two securities be the same. If the prices happen to be different, it could be that one of the securities is overpriced, the other security is underpriced, or the mispricing is a combination of both.

Pairs trading involves selling the higher-priced security and buying the lower-priced security with the idea that the mispricing will correct itself in the future. The mutual mispricing between the two securities is captured by the notion of spread. The greater the spread, the higher the magnitude of mispricing and greater the profit potential. A long–short position in the two securities is constructed such that it has a negligible beta and therefore minimal exposure to the market. Hence, the returns from the trade are uncorrelated to market returns, a feature typical of market neutral strategies.

Based on the discussion so far, it is easy to deduce that the key to success in pairs trading lies in the identification of security pairs. In a study by Gatev et al., a purely empirical approach to achieving this end was adopted. They methodically chose pairs based entirely on the historical price movement of securities and checked to see how pairs trading would have fared in a double-blind study. Besides the set of pairs chosen using historical prices, another set of pairs was created by randomly pairing the securities with one another. The trades that would have been executed based on the empirical pairing approach were then pitted against the trades where the securities were randomly paired. The difference in the returns between the two groups was found to be statistically significant, and the return generated by the methodically paired set was better than the randomly paired sample set.

Unlike the purely empirical approach, the methodology that we subscribe to comprises theoretical valuation concepts that are then validated with empirical models and data. We will later show that the theoretical valuation approach helps us to easily identify pairs based on the fundamentals of the firm. It also leads naturally to the formula used to measure the spread, the degree of mispricing between the two securities. Our theoretical explanation for the comovement of security prices stems from arbitrage pricing theory (APT). According to APT, if two securities have exactly the same risk factor exposures, then the expected return of the two securities for a given time frame is the same. The actual return may, however, differ slightly because of different specific returns for the two securities. It is important to note at this point that APT for the two securities has to be valid in all time frames. Let the price of securities A and B at time t be p_t^A and p_t^B, and at time $t + i$ be p_{t+i}^A and p_{t+i}^B, respectively. The return in the time period i for the two securities is given as $\log(p_t^A) - \log(p_{t+i}^A)$ and $\log(p_t^B) - \log(p_{t+i}^B)$.[1]

Now let us say that we have the prices of both securities at the current time. The return on both securities is expected to be the same in all time frames. In other words, the increment to the logarithm of the prices at the current time must be about the same for both the securities at all time instances in the future. This, of course, means that the time series of the logarithm of the two prices must move together, and the spread calculation formula is therefore based on the difference in the logarithm of the prices.

Having explained our approach, we now need to define in precise terms what we mean when we say that the price series or the log price series of the two securities must move together. Fortunately for us, the idea of comovement of two time series has been well developed in the field of econometrics. We discuss it in the following section on cointegration.

COINTEGRATION

In the introduction to time series we briefly discussed the preprocessing step for nonstationary series. The series is typically transformed into a stationary

---

[1]The value as calculated here is approximately equal to $\dfrac{p_{t+i} - p_t}{p_t}$. Thus, return can be thought of as the increment in the logarithm of the prices.

time series by differencing. By extension, when analyzing multivariate time series where each of the component series is nonstationary, it would then make sense to difference each component and then subject them to examination. However, that need not be the case.

In the course of examining multivariate series to determine statistically if there is a cause–effect relationship between the variables represented by the time series, the econometricians Engle and Granger observed a rather interesting phenomenon. Even though two time series are nonstationary, it is possible that in some instances a specific linear combination of the two is actually stationary; that is, the two series move together in somewhat of a lockstep. Engle and Granger coined the term *cointegration* and proposed the idea in an article, the reference for which is at the end of this chapter. Notably, this was one of the ideas for which they won the Nobel Prize in economics in 2003.

Let us now state the idea of cointegration more formally. Let y_t, and x_t be two nonstationary time series. If for a certain value γ, the series $y_t - \gamma x_t$ is stationary, then the two series are said to be cointegrated. Real-life examples of cointegration abound in economics. In fact, the first demonstrations and tests of cointegration involved economic variable pairs like consumption and income, short-term and long-term rates, the M2 money supply and GDP, and so forth.

The explanation for cointegration dynamics is captured by the notion of error correction. The idea behind error correction is that cointegrated systems have a long-run equilibrium; that is, the long-run mean of the linear combination of the two time series. If there is a deviation from the long-run mean, then one or both time series adjust themselves to restore the long-run equilibrium. The formal theorem stating that error correction and cointegration are essentially equivalent representations is called the Granger representation theorem. We shall not attempt to discuss the proof of the theorem, but simply present here the error correction representation.

Let ε_{x_t} be the white noise process corresponding to time series $\{x_t\}$. Let ε_{y_t} be the white noise process corresponding to the time series $\{y_t\}$. The error correction representation is

$$y_t - y_{t-1} = \alpha_y\left(y_{t-1} - \gamma x_{t-1}\right) + \varepsilon_{y_t} \qquad (5.1)$$

$$x_t - x_{t-1} = \alpha_x\left(y_{t-1} - \gamma x_{t-1}\right) + \varepsilon_{x_t}$$

Let us interpret the Equations 5.1. The left-hand side is the increment to the time series at each time step. The right-hand side is the sum of two expressions, the error correction part and the white noise part. Let us look at the error correction part $\alpha_y(y_{t-1} - \gamma x_{t-1})$ from the first equation. The term $y_{t-1} - \gamma x_{t-1}$ is representative of the deviation from the long-run equilibrium (equilibrium value is zero in this case), and γ is the coefficient of cointegration. α_y is the error correction rate, indicative of the speed with which the time series corrects itself to maintain equilibrium. Thus, as the two series evolve with time, deviations from the long-run equilibrium are caused by white noise, and these deviations are subsequently corrected in future time steps.

We will now illustrate that the idea of error correction does indeed lead to a stationary time series for the spread. Two independent white noise series with zero mean and unit standard deviation were generated to represent ε_{y_t} and ε_{x_t}, respectively. The other values were set as $\alpha_y = -0.2$, $\alpha_x = 0.2$, and $\gamma = 1.0$. Note that it is important to have the two coefficients α_y and α_x set to opposite signs for error-correcting behavior. The values for the two time series $\{x_t\}$ and $\{y_t\}$ were then generated using the simulated data and the equations from the error correction representation. A plot of the two series is shown in Figure 5.1.

Subsequently, the spread at each time instance was calculated using the known value for γ. A plot of the spread series and its autocorrelation is shown in Figures 5.2a and b. It is easy to appreciate from the autocorrelation function that the spread series is indeed stationary.

A more direct approach to model cointegration is attributed to Stock and Watson, called the common trends model. The primary idea of the common

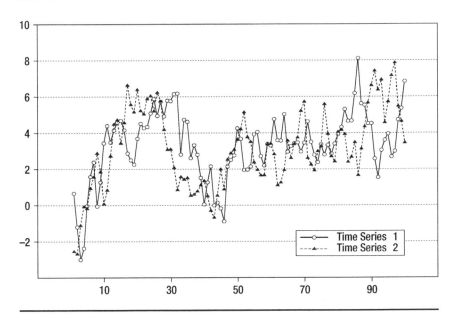

FIGURE 5.1 Cointegrated Time Series.

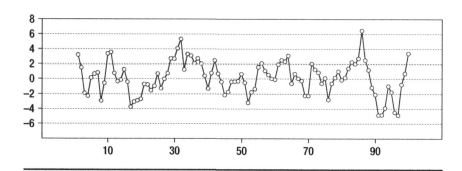

FIGURE 5.2A   Spread.

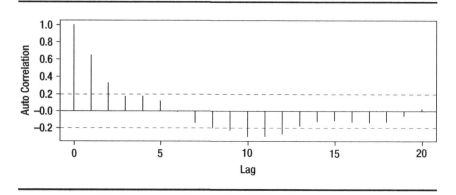

FIGURE 5.2B   Spread ACF.

trends model is that of a time series being expressed as a simple sum of two component time series: a stationary component and a nonstationary component. If two series are cointegrated, then the cointegrating linear composition acts to nullify the nonstationary components, leaving only the stationary components. To see what we mean, consider two time series

$$y_t = n_{y_t} + \varepsilon_{y_t} \qquad (5.2)$$

$$z_t = n_{z_t} + \varepsilon_{z_t}$$

where n_{y_t} and n_{z_t} are the random walk (nonstationary) components of the two time series, and ε_{y_t} and ε_{z_t} are the stationary components of the time series. Also, let the linear combination $y_t - \gamma z_t$ be the cointegrating combination that results in a stationary time series. Expanding the linear combination and rearranging some terms, we have

$$y_t - \gamma z_t = (n_{y_t} - \gamma n_{z_t}) + (\varepsilon_{y_t} - \gamma \varepsilon_{z_t}) \tag{5.3}$$

If the combination in Equation 5.3 must be stationary, the nonstationary component must be zero, implying that $n_{y_t} = \gamma n_{z_t}$, or the trend component of one series must be a scalar multiple of the trend component in the other series. Therefore, for two series to be cointegrated, the trends must be identical up to a scalar. In later chapters, we will rely on the Stock-Watson model to establish links between arbitrage pricing theory and cointegration.

HIGHLIGHTING THE POINT

This is an anecdote about an ingenious little kid. He was asked on a test to say a few sentences about a cow. The poor lad knew only how to say a few sentences about a tree. Thinking for a moment, the kid in his first sentence tied the cow to a tree and then went on to talk about the tree. The example is probably a little tongue in cheek. It is, however, true that there is a strong urge to relate the unknown to something familiar and enhance understanding through association.

To further underscore the point, it is worth mentioning that the spirit of that approach actually forms the basis for formal proof techniques in mathematics. Proof by induction, a technique attributed to Cantor, relies on forming a series of logical relationships from the most general to the most trivial. Proofs of NP completeness, used to classify algorithms in the area of computational complexity theory (attributed to Richard Karp), also rely on transformations to a known problem. It is probably safe to say that in almost all fields of human endeavor there is a common tendency to relate the intractable to something manageable and leverage existing knowledge to arrive at meaningful conclusions.

We are no different from everyone else in this respect. When faced with the prospect of having to work with nonstationary time series, we immediately look for ways to construct portfolios that can be related to stationary time series. The transformation to stationarity is typically achieved using cointegration ideas and strict parity relationships. Needless to say, this approach appears as a recurrent theme in the design of trading strategies across all asset classes.

APPLYING THE MODEL

In this section, we fit the cointegration model to the logarithm of stock prices. For the cointegration model to apply, we would require the logarithm of stock prices to be a nonstationary series. The assumption that the logarithm of stock prices is a random walk (read as nonstationary) is a rather standard one. It has been used fairly extensively in option-pricing models with satisfactory results. We are therefore good on that assumption and ready to proceed further.

Let us say that two stocks A and B are cointegrated with the nonstationary time series corresponding to them being $\left\{\log\left(p_t^A\right)\right\}$ and $\left\{\log\left(p_t^B\right)\right\}$, respectively. Applying the error correction representation described here, we have

$$\log\left(p_t^A\right) - \log\left(p_{t-1}^A\right) = \alpha_A \log\left(p_{t-1}^A\right) - \gamma \log\left(p_{t-1}^B\right) + \varepsilon_A \qquad (5.4)$$

$$\log\left(p_t^B\right) - \log\left(p_{t-1}^B\right) = \alpha_B \log\left(p_{t-1}^A\right) - \gamma \log\left(p_{t-1}^B\right) + \varepsilon_B$$

The parameters that uniquely determine the model are the cointegration coefficient γ and the two error correction constants α_A and α_B. Therefore, estimating the model involves determining the appropriate values for α_A, α_B, and γ. The left-hand side of the Equations 5.4 is the return of the stocks in the current time period. On the right-hand side, note the expression for the long-run equilibrium, $\log(p_{t-1}^A) - \gamma.\log(p_{t-1}^B)$, in both the equations. In words, it is the scaled difference of the logarithm of price. Incidentally, this coincides with what we termed the *spread* in our earlier discussion. Also notice that the subscripts for stock prices in the expression for the long-run equilibrium is $t - 1$. The past deviation from equilibrium plays a role in deciding the next point in the time series. Therefore, knowledge of the past realizations may be used to give us an edge in predicting the increments to the logarithm of prices; that is, returns. This is important and exciting. Even though both stocks follow a log-normal process, one can eke out some predictability in their returns based on past realizations. Thus, one can attempt to trade either of the stocks in the pair based on predictions using the estimated values from the error correction representation.

Let us now focus on the cointegration part of the representation theorem. This is the assertion that the time series of the long-run equilibrium (also termed *spread* in our case) is stationary and mean reverting. Now, we definitely know a lot about predicting stationary time series. If only we could associate the time series of the spread to a portfolio, we could consider trading the portfolio based on our prediction of the time series values. We proceed to do exactly that. Consider a portfolio with long one share of A and short γ shares of B. The return of the portfolio for a given time period is given as

$$\left[\log(p_{t+i}^A) - \log(p_t^A)\right] - \gamma\left[\log(p_{t+i}^B) - \log(p_t^B)\right]. \qquad (5.5)$$

COINTEGRATION AND TRACKING ERROR

Tracking error is an idea that arises naturally in the context of an investment technique called *indexing*. The basic premise for indexing is the notion that it is extremely hard to time the market. Therefore, the strategy adopted is to passively invest in the market index. Alternately, to reduce trading costs, the investment is made in portfolios designed to mimic index returns. These portfolios are sometimes referred to as *tracking baskets*. The ability of the tracking basket to mimic the market returns is characterized by its tracking error. The tracking error may therefore be thought of as a measure of discrepancy or margin of error that one can expect in the tracking process.

Implicit in the definition of tracking error is the time interval for which the returns are measured. It is typically one year (assumed to have 252 trading days). If the holding period is different from one year, then the tracking error needs to be scaled accordingly. The convention is to assume that the tracking error is a random walk series and scale the tracking error using the formula below. If T is the holding period for the portfolio, then

$$\mathrm{err}(T) = \frac{\mathrm{err}(1\ \mathrm{year})}{\sqrt{252}}T \qquad (5.6)$$

The tricky part here is in the random walk assumption for tracking error in the process of scaling. In the case of long–short portfolios consisting of cointegrated stocks, the tracking error is not a random walk series. As a matter of fact, it is a stationary time series. The variance or standard deviation in this case is independent of the holding period. In other words, the tracking error remains the same regardless of the holding period, and scaling formulas are not required.

We therefore caution against making the random walk assumption blindly, particularly in indexing situations, because they tend to distort the tracking error.

Rearranging the terms a little bit, we have

$$\left[\log(p_{t+i}^A) - \gamma \log(p_{t+i}^B)\right] - \left[\log(p_t^A) - \gamma \log(p_t^B)\right] = \text{spread}_{t+i} - \text{spread}_t \quad (5.7)$$

Therefore, the return on the portfolio is the increment to the spread value in the time period i. We have successfully associated a portfolio with a stationary time series. The one thing that remains is providing an interpretation for γ, the cointegration coefficient. We will discuss this in later chapters.

A TRADING STRATEGY

We now construct a simple trading strategy. The idea is to trade on the oscillations about the equilibrium value for the spread. We could put on a trade upon deviation from the equilibrium value and unwind the trade when equilibrium is restored. However, note that the equilibrium value is also the mean value of the time series. Therefore, given that the spread swings equally in both directions about the equilibrium value, we could potentially unwind the trade when the spread deviates in the other direction. This would reduce the trading frequency on average by a factor of two. Given that stocks have a bid-ask spread, we would incur a trading slippage every time a trade is executed. Reducing the trading frequency reduces the effect of this slippage.

Let us therefore consider the strategy where the trades are put on and unwound on a deviation of Δ on either direction from the long-run equilibrium μ. We buy the portfolio (long A and short B) when the time series is Δ below the mean and sell the portfolio (sell A and buy B) when the time series is Δ above the mean in i time steps.

$$\log\left(p_t^A\right) - \gamma \log\left(p_t^B\right) = \mu - \Delta \quad (5.8)$$
$$\log\left(p_{t+i}^A\right) - \gamma \log\left(p_{t+i}^B\right) = \mu + \Delta$$

The profit on the trade is the incremental change in the spread, 2Δ.

Example

The Data
Consider two stocks A and B that are cointegrated with the following data:

Cointegration Ratio = 1.5
Delta used for trade signal = 0.045
Bid price of A at time t = \$19.50
Ask price of B at time t = \$7.46

Ask price of A at time $t + i = \$20.10$
Bid price of B at time $t + i = \$7.17$
Average bid-ask spread for A = .0005 percent (5 basis points)
Average bid-ask spread for B = .0010 percent (10 basis points)

The Strategy

We first examine if trading is feasible given the average bid-ask spreads.

Average trading slippage = ($0.0005 + 1.5 \times 0.0010$)
$$= .002 (20 \text{ basis points})$$

This is smaller than the delta value of 0.045. Trading is therefore feasible. At time t, buy shares of A and short shares of B in the ratio 1:1.5.

Spread at time t $= \log (19.50) - 1.5 \times \log (7.46)$
$$= -0.045$$

At time $t + i$, sell shares of A and buy back shares the shares of B.

Spread at time $t + i$ $= \log (20.10) - 1.5 \times \log (7.17)$
$$= 0.045$$

Total return = return on A + $\gamma \times$ return on B

$$= \log (20.10) - \log(19.50) + 1.5 \times (\log(7.46) - \log(7.17))$$
$$= 0.3 + 1.5 \times 4.0$$
$$= .09 \text{ (9 percent)}$$

ROAD MAP FOR STRATEGY DESIGN

The discussion so far briefly outlines how we might trade once we know two stocks are cointegrated. We do concede that the course of the discussion so far has brought up more questions on the details. How do we identify candidate stock pairs? Can we verify that they are indeed cointegrated? How do we determine the cointegration coefficient? What is the most appropriate value for delta? We explore the questions and issues involved in the subsequent chapters. To that end, we provide a road map for the design and analysis of the pairs trading strategy.

The steps involved are as follows:

1. Identify stock pairs that could potentially be cointegrated. This process can be based on the stock fundamentals or alternately on a pure statistical approach based on historical data. Our preferred approach is to make the stock pair guesses using fundamental information.

2. Once the potential pairs are identified, we verify the proposed hypothesis that the stock pairs are indeed cointegrated based on statistical evidence from historical data. This involves determining the cointegration coefficient and examining the spread time series to ensure that it is stationary and mean reverting.
3. We then examine the cointegrated pairs to determine the delta. A feasible delta that can be traded on will be substantially greater than the slippage encountered due to the bid-ask spreads in the stocks. We also indicate methods to compute holding periods.

SUMMARY

- Statistical pairs trading is a relative value arbitrage on two securities and is based on the premise that there is a long-run equilibrium between the prices of the stocks composing the pair.
- The degree of deviation from the long-run equilibrium is called the *spread* and represents the extent of mutual mispricing.
- Any deviation from the long-run equilibrium is compensated for in subsequent movements of the time series.
- Pairs trading involves trading on the oscillations about the equilibrium value.
- The econometric paradigm of cointegration and error correction is central to the analysis of the pairs-trading strategy.

FURTHER READING MATERIAL

Pairs Trading

Gatev, Evan, G., William, N. Goetzmann, and K. Greet Rouwenhorst. *Pairs Trading: Performance of a Relative Value Arbitrage Rule*. NBER Working Papers 7032, National Bureau of Economic Research Inc., 1999.

Cointegration

Engle, Robert F. and C. W. Granger. "Co-integration and Error Correction: Representation, Estimation and Testing." *Econometrica* 55, no. 2 (March 1987): 251–276.
Stock, James H. and Mark W. Watson. "Testing for Common Trends." *Journal of the American Statistical Association* 83, no. 404 (December 1988): 1097–1107.
Enders, Walter. *Applied Econometric Time Series*. (New York: John Wiley & Sons, Inc., 1995).

CHAPTER 6

Pairs Selection in Equity Markets

INTRODUCTION

In Chapter 5, we explained that strategy design was essentially a three-step process. The three steps are identification of stock pairs, cointegration testing, and trading rule formulation. In this chapter, we focus on the first of the three steps, the process of identifying potential stock pairs. In this step we essentially short-list the pairs for cointegration testing and further analysis. Why do we need to do that? We could just as well work with a candidate list of all possible pairs, run cointegration tests on all of them, and eliminate pairs that fail the tests. This certainly seems reasonable, except for the fact that in a universe of 5,000 stocks, we have a total of about 12 million pairs.

Running tests on 12 million pairs is definitely not a viable option. Therefore, the natural inclination is to try to reduce the number.

The most expedient way (not necessarily the best) to accomplish that is by using heuristics, or rules of thumb. In the heuristics approach, the list of pairs is explicitly partitioned into two sets: potentially cointegrated and not potentially cointegrated. This partitioning is accomplished by applying a set of rules. The rules are designed to exclude pairs with a slim chance of being cointegrated. This limits the number of pairs in the candidate list and reduces the number of cointegration tests that need to be performed. Although this approach seems reasonable, it is best characterized as being ad hoc. Different people have different belief systems about the market. Therefore, reasonable people can come up with dramatically different rule sets based on their personal experiences. This makes the rule sets anecdotal in nature. Furthermore, it is possible for individuals to hold opposing views. An aggregation of rules representing the beliefs of multiple individuals may end up being inconsistent. This is now a case where the whole is lesser than the sum of its parts and results in missed opportunities. It might therefore be useful to put some thought into this to come up with a more definitive methodology.

The methodology we prescribe here is distinctly different from the rules of thumb or heuristics approach. Instead of attempting to evaluate explicit partitions, this approach aims to arrive at a relative ordering of the pairs based on the degree of comovement. Each pair is associated with a score/distance measure. The higher the score, the greater the degree of comovement, and vice versa. Notably, such a structure lends itself to deductive reasoning. If we find that a pair is unsuitable for pairs trading, then we have good reason to believe that every pair with a score/distance measure worse than the current pair is also unsuitable. The pair selection process now becomes equivalent to choosing a suitable threshold value for the distance measure. Notice that this approach relies solely on the distance measure for ordering the pairs. Therefore, a proper choice of the distance measure is key to the pairs selection process.

Let us quickly examine the properties that would be desirable of the score/distance measure. First, if the evaluation of the score/distance measure took as much effort as cointegration testing, then it would defeat the purpose. We may as well test for cointegration directly with all the pairs in the exhaustive list. Therefore, at the very least, the evaluation of the distance measure must be relatively easy and straightforward. Additionally, it is desirable that the distance measure not be completely empirical. Empirical deductions rely solely on historical data. This comes with an underlying assumption that the fundamentals of the firm are essentially static. There are no changes that impact the valuation of the firm. Needless to say, this need not be true. Ideally, we would prefer to tie the evaluation of the distance measure to the fundamentals of the firm. Accomplishing this would help provide a theoretical justification for the use of the score/distance measure and therefore a sound economic rationale for our expectation of cointegrated behavior.

In this chapter, we focus on defining, justifying, and interpreting the score/distance measure. It is therefore a bit theoretical in nature. To help motivate the choice of the score/distance measure, the nexus between cointegration and arbitrage pricing theory (APT) is explored. We draw parallels between the common trends model for cointegration and the ideas of APT. Conditions to be satisfied for cointegration in the common trends model are translated into APT constructs. This makes it possible to evaluate the score/distance measure in the APT framework. Moreover, if the multifactor implementation of APT is composed of fundamental variables, then the distance measure calculated relates to the fundamentals of the firm. We will then have an easy evaluation procedure for the distance measure that is firmly based on the fundamentals of the firm, thus satisfying the requirements of the score/distance measure.

In addition, we bridge the gap between theoretical expectations and practical observations. Assumptions, caveats, and loopholes that are encountered in the process are stated explicitly. Insights gained in the exercise will help us understand what can go wrong and the things to beware of while trading. Sources of risk are identified and quantified with a view to enhance the understanding of the dynamics involved in pairs trading and the kinds of pairs to avoid. Let us start with the common trends model.

COMMON TRENDS COINTEGRATION MODEL

Let us recall the common trends model from Chapter 5. We are given two series y_t and z_t, as shown in Equation 6.1.

$$y_t = n_{y_t} + \varepsilon_{y_t} \qquad (6.1)$$
$$z_t = n_{z_t} + \varepsilon_{z_t}$$

n_{y_t} and n_{z_t} represent the so-called common trends or random walk components of the two time series; $\varepsilon_{y_t}, \varepsilon_{z_t}$ are the stationary and specific components of the time series. If the two series are cointegrated, then their common trends must be identical up to a scalar,

$$n_{y_t} = \gamma n_{z_t} \qquad (6.2)$$

where γ is the cointegration coefficient. Let us examine some of the implications of the common trends model.

Inference 1: **In a cointegrated system with two time series, the innovations sequences derived from the common trend components must be perfectly correlated. (Correlation value must be +1 or –1).**

Let us denote the innovation sequences derived from the common trends of the two series as r_{y_t} and r_{z_t}. Recall from Chapter 2 that the innovation sequence for a random walk is obtained by differencing it. The innovation sequences shown here are therefore the result of differencing n_{yt} and n_{zt}, respectively. In equation form, we have

$$n_{y_{t+1}} - n_{y_t} = r_{y_{t+1}} \qquad (6.3)$$

$$n_{z_{t+1}} - n_{z_t} = r_{z_{t+1}}$$

According to the common trends model, the common trends must be identical up to a scalar.

$$n_{y_t} = \gamma n_{z_t} \qquad (6.4)$$

Now, if we require

$$n_{y_{t+1}} = \gamma n_{z_{t+1}} \qquad (6.5)$$

it follows from simple algebra on Equations 6.4 and 6.5 that

$$r_{y_{t+1}} = \gamma r_{z_{t+1}} \qquad (6.6)$$

This means that the innovations derived from the common trends must also be identical up to a scalar. Incidentally, the scalar also happens to be the cointegration coefficient γ. Now, if two variables are identical up to a scalar (in this case the cointegration coefficient), they must be perfectly correlated. If the cointegration coefficient is positive, then the correlation value is +1. If it is negative, then the correlation value is –1.

Thus, in a cointegrated system the innovation sequences derived from the common trends must be perfectly correlated.

Inference 2: **The cointegration coefficient may be obtained by a regression of the innovation sequences of the common trends against each other.**

Based on the preceding discussion we have a linear relationship between the innovation sequences given as

$$r_{y_t} = \gamma r_{z_t} \qquad (6.7)$$

It therefore follows that the cointegration coefficient may be obtained by performing a simple regression of one innovation sequence against the other. The cointegration coefficient is therefore given as

$$\gamma = \frac{\text{cov}\left(r_y, r_z\right)}{\text{var}\left(r_z\right)} \tag{6.8}$$

Discussion

In this section we looked at conditions necessary for cointegration. We established that the innovation sequences derived from the common trend terms must be perfectly correlated. We urge the reader to take special note of this fact. The idea resonates throughout the chapter and forms the basis for the scoring function.

A subtle point to highlight at this juncture is that there are in effect two correlation measures. One correlation measure pertains to the innovation sequences of the common trend alone. This correlation value is either +1 or −1. Another correlation may be calculated on the innovation sequences of the whole series, taking into account both the common trend and the stationary components. This measure can take on a whole range of values depending on the variance of the stationary components. The two correlation measures are very different, and it important not to confuse one for the other.

Our next point pertains to the stationarity of the common trend and specific components of the two time series. As far as common trends go, there is no restriction on them. They can be stationary or nonstationary, and this is neither critical nor material for cointegration. The same cannot be said for the specific components. The definition of the common trends model relies on their being stationary time series. Therefore, for cointegration to exist, it is absolutely necessary for the specific components to be stationary. By implication, the first difference of the specific component must not be white noise, because if the differenced series were white noise, then the specific series would be a random walk, a nonstationary series. This violates the stationarity condition for the specific component. Therefore, the first difference of the specific component cannot be white noise.

In summary, there are two conditions that need to be satisfied for cointegration in a common trends model. First, the innovation sequences derived from the common trends of the two series must be identical up to a scalar. Next, the specific components of the two series must be stationary. Having now established an understanding of the common trends model, we turn to the issue of applying this to stock data. Application is possible only if we separate the time series into nonstationary/common trends and stationary/specific components. To do that, we look to arbitrage pricing theory (APT) and establish a link between APT and the common trends model. This will be the focus of the discussion in the following section, on common trends.

COMMON TRENDS MODEL AND APT

Earlier, in Chapter 2, the logarithm of stock price was modeled as a random walk. To accommodate the common trends model, let us modify that a little and consider the logarithm of the stock price to be a sum of a random walk and a stationary series

$$\log(\text{price}_t) = n_t + \varepsilon_t \qquad (6.9)$$

where n_t is the random walk, and ε_t is the stationary component. Differencing the logarithm of stock price yields the sequence of returns. Therefore, based on Equation 6.9, the return r_t at time t may also be separated into two parts

$$\log(price_t) - \log(price_{t-1}) = n_t - n_{t-1} + (\varepsilon_t - \varepsilon_{t-1}) \qquad (6.10)$$

$$r_t = r_t^c + r_t^s \qquad (6.11)$$

where r_t^c is the return due to the nonstationary trend component, and r_t^s is the return due to the stationary component.

Notice that the return due to trend component is the same as the innovation derived from the trend component. Therefore, the cointegration criterion pertaining to the innovations of the common trend may be rephrased as follows: If two stocks are cointegrated, the returns from their common trends must be identical up to a scalar. But why in the world should stocks ever have common returns? Is there a financial rationale for these to exist among stocks? The answer to that is a resounding yes, and APT comes in handy in providing a comprehensive explanation for this. Recalling the earlier discussions on APT, stock returns may be separated into common factor returns (returns based on the exposure of stocks to different risk factors) and specific returns (returns specific to the stock). If two stocks share the same risk factor exposure profile, then the common factor returns for both the stocks must be the same. This provides us with a rationale for when we might expect stocks to have a common return component.

We are now ready to draw parallels between the common trends model and APT. According to APT, stock returns for a time period may be separated into two types: common factor returns and specific returns. Let these correspond to the common trend innovation and the first difference of the specific component in the common trends model. For the correspondence to be valid, the integration of the specific returns must be a stationary time series.

Alternately, as discussed in the previous section, the specific returns must not be white noise. But APT is a single time frame model and cannot provide us with any guarantees on the time series of specific returns. We would therefore have to make that leap of faith and assume that the specific return series is not white noise. Nevertheless, it is reassuring to know that the validity of this assumption is tested when running the cointegration tests and pairs where the specific component is nonstationary are eliminated.

Let us go ahead and make the assumption that the specific return is not white noise. We can now interpret the inferences from the common trends model in APT terms. The correlation of the innovation sequence is the common factor correlation. Also, the cointegration coefficient may be calculated using APT constructs to evaluate the common factor variance and covariance in its formula. Let us now formally put all of the preceding discussions into an observation.

Observation 1: **A pair of stocks with the same risk factor exposure profile satisfies the necessary conditions for cointegration.**

Condition 1

Now let us consider two stocks A and B with risk factor exposure vectors γx and x, respectively. The factor exposure vectors in this case are identical up to a scalar. We denote the factor exposures as

Stock A: $\qquad\qquad \gamma x = (\gamma x_1, \gamma x_2, \gamma x_3, ..., \gamma x_n)$

Stock B: $\qquad\qquad x = (x_1, x_2, x_3, ..., x_n)$

Geometrically, it may be interpreted that the factor exposure vectors of the two stocks point in the same direction; that is, the angle between them is zero.

If $b = (b_1, b_2, b_3, ..., b_n)$ is the factor returns vector, and r_A^{spec} and r_B^{spec} are the specific returns for stocks A and B, then the returns for the stocks r_A and r_B are given as

$$r_A = \gamma \left(x_1 b_1 + x_2 b_2 + x_3 b_3 +, ..., + b_n \right) + r_A^{\text{spec}}$$
$$r_B = \left(x_1 b_1 + x_2 b_2 + x_3 b_3 +, ..., + x_n b_n \right) + r_B^{\text{spec}}$$

The common factor returns for the stocks are therefore

$$r_A^{cf} = \gamma\left(x_1 b_1 + x_2 b_2 + x_3 b_3 +, \dots, + x_n b_n\right)$$
$$r_B^{cf} = x_1 b_1 + x_2 b_2 + x_3 b_3 +, \dots, + x_n b_n$$

Thus, $r_A^{cf} = \gamma r_B^{cf}$. The innovation sequences of the common trend are identical up to a scalar. This satisfies the first condition for cointegration as per the common trends model.

Condition 2
Now consider the linear combination of the returns.

$$r_A - \gamma r_B = \left(r_A^{cf} - \gamma r_B^{cf}\right) + \left(r_A^{spec} - \gamma r_B^{spec}\right)$$

The left-hand side of the equation represents the return of a portfolio long one share of A and short γ shares of B. The right-hand side shows that this return is separable into common factor returns and specific returns of the portfolio. Therefore

$$r_{port} = r_{port}^{cf} + r_{port}^{spec}$$

where

$$r_{port}^{cf} = r_A^{cf} - \gamma r_B^{cf}$$
$$r_{port}^{spec} = r_A^{spec} - \gamma r_B^{spec}$$

Notice that if the stocks A and B are cointegrated, then the common factor return r_{port}^{cf} becomes zero.

Additionally, the return on the long–short portfolio may also be viewed as the output from differencing the spread time series. Based on the separation of the return series, the spread series may also be represented as the sum of two components. One is the integrated common factor return, which we shall call the common factor spread. The other is the integrated specific return, which we shall call the specific spread. Writing this in equation form, we have

$$spread_t^{cf} - spread_{t-1}^{cf} = r_{port}^{cf}$$
$$spread_t^{spec} - spread_{t-1}^{spec} = r_{port}^{spec}$$
$$spread_t^{port} = spread_t^{cf} + spread_t^{spec}$$

Again notice that if the stocks are cointegrated, then $spread_t^{cf}$ becomes zero, because r_{port}^{cf} is zero. Therefore, when the stocks are cointegrated, the spread of the portfolio is the same as the spread due to the specific components.

Additionally, the spread series must be stationary for cointegration. This will be true if the spread due to specific spread is stationary. The specific spread will be stationary if the integration of the specific returns of the individual specific returns of the stocks is stationary. This is indeed the assumption that we make when relating APT with cointegration. Therefore, if this assumption bears out, we will have satisfied all the necessary conditions for cointegration.

Summary

The driving idea in the common trends model has been to view a given time series as a sum of stationary and nonstationary components. The idea of viewing a time series as a sum of component series for ease of analysis is in fact a common practice. Notably, in the practical analysis of time series, the convention is to make an implicit assumption that the series is composed of trend, seasonal, and stochastic components. Arbitrage pricing theory declares this idea of composition rather explicitly and takes on a constructionist approach to modeling stock returns. Every risk factor in the APT model is associated with a time series of returns. The weighted sum of these series, with the factor exposures as weights, is the expected returns series for a stock. To get the actual returns, we need to add the specific return series to the expected returns.

Two stocks with identical risk factor exposures would therefore have the same common factor returns. In other words, the common factor return of a long–short portfolio of the two stocks is zero. The common factor contribution to risk in this case is the least it can ever be, zero. Furthermore, if the integration of the specific returns of the stocks is stationary, then the two stocks are cointegrated. Thus, a key area to look for a measure of cointegration is the risk factor exposure profiles of the stocks and how closely aligned they are.

THE DISTANCE MEASURE

We are now ready to define the distance measure. Recall from the discussions on the common trends model that the necessary condition for cointegration is that the innovation sequences derived from the common trends must be perfectly correlated. We also established that the common factor return of the APT model might be interpreted as the innovations derived from the common trends. The correlation between the innovation sequences is therefore the correlation between the common factor returns. The closer the absolute value of this measure is to unity, the greater will be the degree of comovement. The distance measure we propose is therefore exactly that: the absolute value of the correlation of the common factor returns.

The formula for the distance measure is therefore given as

$$d(A, B) = |\rho| = \left| \frac{\text{cov}(r_A, r_B)}{\sqrt{\text{var}(r_A)\,\text{var}(r_B)}} \right| \tag{6.12}$$

In APT terms, if x_A and x_B are the factor exposure vectors of the two stocks A and B, and F is the covariance matrix, the distance measure may be calculated as

$$|\rho| = \left| \frac{x_A F x_B}{\sqrt{(x_A F x_B)(x_B F x_B)}} \right| \tag{6.13}$$

Note that in Equation 6.13 we have used only common factor terms. The specific variance contribution is not used.

INTERPRETING THE DISTANCE MEASURE

In previous discussions we hinted that the perfect alignment of the factor exposure vectors, that is, a zero angle between them, is indicative of cointegration. In this section we will show that the correlation measure as calculated in Equation 6.13 could actually be interpreted as the cosine of the angle between transformed versions of the factor exposure vectors corresponding to the two stocks.

But why do we need to transform the factor exposure vectors? Can we not directly measure the angle between them? We could do that but for the fact that all factors in the multifactor model are not created equal. Returns are more sensitive to changes in some factors versus the others. We therefore need to transform from the space of factor exposure to the space of returns and then measure the angle between the transformed vectors. We will discuss the exact nature of this transformation and show that correlation can indeed be interpreted as the cosine of the angle.

Calculating the Cosine of the Angle between Two Vectors

It is useful at this point to define the inner product of two vectors. Given two vectors e_A and e_B as follows:

$$e_A = \left(e_1^A, e_2^A, \ldots, e_N^A\right) \qquad (6.14)$$

$$e_B = \left(e_1^B, e_2^B, \ldots, e_N^B\right)$$

The inner product between the two vectors is given by the formula

$$e_A e_B = e_1^A e_1^B + e_2^A e_2^B + \ldots + e_N^A e_N^B \qquad (6.15)$$

In matrix notation, the inner product may be represented as $e_A e_B^T$, where e_B^T is the transpose of the vector. The length of a vector is the square root of its inner product. Therefore, we have

$$\text{length}\left(e_A\right) = \sqrt{e_A e_A^T} \qquad (6.16)$$

With the preceding equations, we are now ready to calculate the angle between two vectors. The steps involved in calculating the angle between two vectors are as follows.

Step 1. We first evaluate the unit vectors (vectors of length one) pointing in the direction of the two vectors. We do this by scaling each element of the vector by its length.

Step 2. The cosine of the angle between the two vectors is now the inner product of the unit vectors pointing in their directions.

We will leave it to the reader to work out that the two steps may be condensed into a single formula as given in Equation 6.17.

$$\cos \theta = \frac{e_A e_B^T}{\sqrt{\left(e_A e_A^T\right)\left(e_B e_B^T\right)}} \qquad (6.17)$$

Example

Let us say we are required to calculate the cosine of the angle between the vectors $A = (0, 2)$ and $B = (3, 0)$. Calculating the lengths of these vectors, we have

$$\text{length}(A) = \sqrt{0^2 + 2^2} = 2$$
$$\text{length}(B) = \sqrt{3^2 + 0^2} = 3$$

We now scale each vector by dividing every element in the vector by the length of the vector. Denoting the unit vectors in small letters, we have

$$a = (0, 1)$$
$$b = (1, 0)$$

The cosine of the angle between the vectors is given by the inner product of the unit vectors.

$$\cos\theta = ab = 0.1 + 1.0 = 0$$

The value of the cosine is zero, indicating that the angle between the two vectors is 90 degrees. The two vectors are indeed orthogonal to each other.

Geometric Interpretation

Key to doing the geometric interpretation is the idea of eigenvalue decomposition of the covariance matrix F. A brief discussion on eigenvalue decomposition is provided in the appendix. Let the eigenvalue decomposition of F be given as UDU^T. If x_A and x_B are the factor exposure vectors of the two stocks, let us consider a transformation of the two vectors as shown in Equations 6.18.

$$e_A = x_A UD^{1/2} \tag{6.18}$$
$$e_B = x_B UD^{1/2}$$

This is the transformation from the factor exposure space to the factor return space. Now, using simple matrix manipulations it is easy to verify that

$$\text{length}(e_A) = \sqrt{x_A F x_A^T} = \sqrt{\text{var}(r_A)} \tag{6.19}$$

$$\text{length}(e_B) = \sqrt{x_B F x_B^T} = \sqrt{\text{var}(r_B)} \tag{6.20}$$

$$e_A e_B^T = x_A F x_B^T = \text{cov}(r_A, r_B) \tag{6.21}$$

Using Equations 6.19, 6.18, and 6.19, the cosine of the angle between the vectors e_A and e_B works out as follows:

$$\cos \theta = \frac{e_A e_B^T}{\sqrt{\text{length}(e_A)\text{length}(e_B)}} = \frac{x_A F x_B^T}{\sqrt{\left(x_A F x_A^T\right)\left(x_B F x_B^T\right)}} = \quad (6.22)$$

$$= \frac{\text{cov}\left(r_A, r_B\right)}{\sqrt{\text{var}\left(r_A\right)\text{var}\left(r_B\right)}} = \rho$$

This completes the geometric interpretation.

RECONCILING THEORY AND PRACTICE

So far we have established the basis for the distance measure in theory. We have shown that the absolute value of the common factor correlation is a good way to measure the degree of comovement in stock prices. Let us now examine the practical issues surrounding it. There may be issues and sources of error that we may not be able to mitigate entirely. However, being aware of them and the risks they pose can provide insights into what can go wrong during trading.

Stationarity of Integrated Specific Returns

We discussed earlier that the necessary condition for cointegration is that the integration of the specific returns time series must be stationary. To verify this directly means that we must evaluate the common factor and specific returns for each time period. Alternately, this could be verified when performing the cointegration tests.

Cointegration testing involves the estimation of the cointegration coefficient and ensuring that the spread series of the long–short portfolio constructed with this ratio is indeed stationary. If the integration of the spread series is nonstationary, this would show up in the spread series being nonstationary. Readers can convince themselves of this by examining the observation made in the section *Common Trends Model and APT*. Thus, testing for stationarity of the spread is sufficient to ensure that stationarity of the integrated specific returns, and the assumption that we make here is verified in due course.

Deviations from Ideal Conditions

From an APT point of view we established that two stocks will be cointegrated if their factor exposure vectors are perfectly aligned. More precisely, the common factor correlation between them must be +1 or −1. This is a rather tall order and is seldom satisfied in practice. Unless the stocks are class A and class B shares of the same firm, it is unlikely that the stocks' factor exposures will be perfectly aligned.

If two stocks do not have their factor exposures perfectly aligned, then any long–short portfolio composed of the two stocks will have a nonzero component for the common factor returns. Our model for cointegration relies on a zero value for the common factor returns, and the violation of this represents deviation from ideal conditions for cointegration. Stating the above in formula form, we have

$$r_A - \gamma r_B = \left(r_A^{cf} - \gamma r_B^{cf} \right) + \left(r_A^{spec} - \gamma r_B^{spec} \right) \qquad (6.23)$$

$$r_{portf} = r_{port}^{cf} + r_{port}^{cf} \qquad (6.24)$$

The value of r_{port}^{cf} in Equation 6.24 is nonzero. Consequently, following the logic from the observation in the section *Common Trends and APT*, the common factor spread is also a nonzero quantity. It is helpful to write this in equation form.

$$spread_t = spread_t^{cf} + spread_t^{spec} \qquad (6.25)$$

The common factor spread may very well be nonstationary, violating the cointegration condition of spread stationarity. But can we still make do with less than perfect conditions of cointegration? How do we quantify the deviation? Let us say that the spread series is composed of a stationary component (typically the specific spread) and a nonstationary component (typically the common factor spread). Let the variances of the two components be $\sigma_{stationary}^2$ and $\sigma_{nonstationary,T}^2$. Note that the variance of the nonstationary component is specified for a time horizon T. Also, let t be the trading horizon. If the change in the nonstationary component of the spread is small, we could treat it more or less as a constant and say that we have a cointegrated pair. A measure of the deviation from cointegration is captured in the signal-to-noise ratio as given in Equation 6.26.

$$SNR = \frac{\sigma_{stationary}}{\sigma_{nonstationary,t}} \qquad (6.26)$$

The ideal is to have the nonstationary component as close to zero as possible. If it is exactly zero, then the signal-to-noise ratio would be infinity. In practice, a very large number for the ratio would make our assumption of cointegration reasonable. Given that the variance of the nonstationary component increases linearly with the trading horizon, then, all things being equal, having a shorter trading horizon is definitely closer to the ideal condition of cointegration. This is of course determined by the dynamics of the spread and the rate at which the spread oscillates about the mean.

Based on Equation 6.25, the overall spread may also be interpreted as the specific return spread with a varying mean that is dictated by the common factor spread. If the common factor spread is a nonstationary time series, then the overall spread is equal to the specific spread with a stochastic drift to its mean value. Thus, deviation from ideal cointegration conditions results in what we shall call *mean drift*. The fallout from mean drift is that trading with symmetric bands may not be optimal because the movement of the spread series may be skewed. The worse part is that it could skew either way depending on the movement of the common factor spread, and it is not possible to know in advance. Also, if the common factor spread is nonstationary, then the variance of the skew scales linearly with time. An important insight to be gleaned in the process is that the mere passage of time represents an increase in risk in pairs trading and must be taken into account to design time-based stop orders.

Model Error

Model error occurs when our model specification is way off the mark. Let us say that there is dramatic news that could potentially result in a drastic change in fundamentals of a firm. The market immediately begins the process of adjustment to the news, predicting in some sense where the factor exposures of the firm would be under the new circumstances.

In such cases where the expectation is for a dramatic change in the factor exposure, the common factor correlation evaluated before becomes dated, and the correlation structure between the two stocks breaks down. It is important to be aware of this and be constantly on the lookout for such events when trading pairs.

Numerical Example

Consider three stocks *A*, *B*, and *C* with factor exposures in a two factor model as follows:

$$x_A = [1 \quad 1]$$
$$x_B = [0.75 \quad 1]$$
$$x_C = [1 \quad 0.75]$$

Let the factor covariance matrix $F = \begin{bmatrix} .0625 & .0225 \\ .0225 & .1024 \end{bmatrix}$

Step 1: Calculate the common factor variance and covariance.

$$\text{var}(A) = \begin{bmatrix} 1 & 1 \end{bmatrix} \begin{bmatrix} .0625 & .0225 \\ .0225 & .1024 \end{bmatrix} \begin{bmatrix} 1 \\ 1 \end{bmatrix} = .2099$$

(sqrt(.2099) is the volatility, 45.8%)

$$\text{var}(B) = \begin{bmatrix} .75 & 1 \end{bmatrix} \begin{bmatrix} .0625 & .0225 \\ .0225 & .1024 \end{bmatrix} \begin{bmatrix} 0.75 \\ 1 \end{bmatrix} = .171 \text{ (volatility of 41.3\%)}$$

$$\text{var}(C) = \begin{bmatrix} 1 & .75 \end{bmatrix} \begin{bmatrix} .0625 & .0225 \\ .0225 & .1024 \end{bmatrix} \begin{bmatrix} 1 \\ .75 \end{bmatrix} = .1539 \text{ (volatility of 39.2\%)}$$

$$\text{cov}(A, B) = \begin{bmatrix} 1 & 1 \end{bmatrix} \begin{bmatrix} .0625 & .0225 \\ .0225 & .1024 \end{bmatrix} \begin{bmatrix} .75 \\ 1 \end{bmatrix} = .1887$$

$$\text{cov}(A, C) = \begin{bmatrix} 1 & 1 \end{bmatrix} \begin{bmatrix} .0625 & .0225 \\ .0225 & .1024 \end{bmatrix} \begin{bmatrix} 1 \\ .75 \end{bmatrix} = .1787$$

Step 2: Calculate the correlation (absolute value of correlation is the distance measure).

$$\text{corr}(A, B) = \frac{\text{cov}(A, B)}{\sqrt{\text{var}(A)\,\text{var}(B)}} = \frac{0.1887}{\sqrt{.2099 \times .171}} = 0.9957$$

$$\text{corr}(A, C) = \frac{\text{cov}(A, C)}{\sqrt{\text{var}(A)\,\text{var}(C)}} = \frac{0.1787}{\sqrt{.2099 \times .171539}} = 0.9431$$

If we have to choose one pair for purposes of trading, based on the distance measure, our choice would therefore be the pair (A, B).

Step 3: Calculate the cointegration coefficient. A detailed discussion on the reasoning for the formula is provided in the next chapter.

$$\lambda_{AB} = \frac{\text{cov}(AB)}{\text{var}(B)} = \frac{.1887}{.171} = 1.1032$$

$$\lambda_{AC} = \frac{\text{cov}(AC)}{\text{var}(C)} = \frac{.1787}{.1539} = 1.1613$$

Step 4: Calculate the residual common factor exposure in the paired portfolio. This is the exposure that causes mean drift.

$$\exp_{AB} = [1 \quad 1] - 1.1032 \times [0.75 \quad 1] = [.1726 \quad -.1032]$$

$$\exp_{AC} = [1 \quad 1] - 1.1613 \times [1 \quad .75] = [-.1613 \quad .129]$$

Step 5. Calculate the common factor portfolio variance/variance of residual exposure.

$$\text{var}\left(r_{AB}^{cf}\right) = \begin{bmatrix} .1726 & -.1032 \end{bmatrix} \begin{bmatrix} .0625 & .0225 \\ .0225 & .1024 \end{bmatrix} \begin{bmatrix} .1726 \\ -.1032 \end{bmatrix} = .0221$$

$$\sigma_{AB}^{cf} = \sqrt{.0021} = .046$$

$$\text{var}\left(r_{AC}^{cf}\right) = \begin{bmatrix} -.1613 & .129 \end{bmatrix} \begin{bmatrix} .0625 & .0225 \\ .0225 & .1024 \end{bmatrix} \begin{bmatrix} -.1613 \\ .129 \end{bmatrix} = .0024$$

$$\sigma_{AC}^{cf} = \sqrt{.0024} = .049$$

Step 6. Calculate the specific variance of the portfolio.
To simplify our illustration, let us assume the specific variance for all of the stocks to be 0.0016.

$$\text{var}\left(r_{AB}^{spec}\right) = \text{var}\left(r_{A}^{spec}\right) + \gamma_{AB}^2 \text{var}\left(r_{B}^{spec}\right)$$
$$= .0016 + 1.1032^2 \times .0016 = .0035$$

$$\sigma_{AB}^{spec} = \sqrt{.00035} = .059$$

$$\text{var}\left(r_{AC}^{spec}\right) = \text{var}\left(r_{A}^{spec}\right) + \gamma_{AC}^2 \text{var}\left(r_{C}^{spec}\right)$$
$$= .0016 + 1.1613^2 \times .0016 = .0037$$

$$\sigma_{AB}^{spec} = \sqrt{.0037} = .061$$

Step 7. Calculate the SNR ratio with white noise assumptions for residual stock return.

$$SNR_{AB} = \frac{\sigma_{AB}^{spec}}{\sigma_{AB}^{cf}} = \frac{.059}{.046} = 1.282$$

$$SNR_{AC} = \frac{\sigma_{AC}^{spec}}{\sigma_{AC}^{cf}} = \frac{.061}{.049} = 1.245$$

Therefore, even on a signal-to-noise ratio basis the stock pair (A B) does better than stock pair (A C). Notice that having a high value for the specific risk/variance (provided it is stationary) is highly desirable as it improves the *SNR*. A higher specific variance means higher stock volatility, indicating that a high volatility environment is conducive for pairs trading.

SUMMARY

■ The candidate list of potentially cointegrated stock pairs can be compiled by the process of identifying similar stocks.
■ The notion of similarity is formalized using a distance measure between two stocks.
■ The distance measure is based on an APT model possibly with fundamental risk factors.
■ The candidate list of pairs is determined by choosing pairs with distance values within a certain threshold.
■ The distance measure is the absolute value of the common factor correlation between the two stocks.
■ If the common factor correlation is +1 or –1 and the integration of the specific return series of the stocks involved are stationary, then conditions for cointegration are satisfied.
■ It may be possible to trade pairs of stocks even though they deviate from ideal conditions of cointegration.
■ The signal-to-noise ratio as defined is a measure of the deviation from the ideal condition of cointegration.

FURTHER READING MATERIAL

Cointegration Properties

Philips, P. C. B. and S. N. Durlauf. "Multiple Time Series Regression with Integrated Processes," *Review of Economic Studies* 53 (1986): 473–495.
Park, J. Y. S. Oularis and B. Choi. "Spurious Regressions and Tests for Co-integration" (CAE working paper 88–07, Cornell University, Ithaca, New York (1988).)

Near Cointegration

Haldrup, Niels and Michael Jansson. "Spurious Regression, Co-integration and Near Co-integration: A Unifying Approach" (working papers, DK-8000, Department of Economics, University of Aarhus, Denmark, 1999.)

APPENDIX: EIGENVALUE DECOMPOSITION

Consider a scalar λ and a corresponding vector v. They are an eigenvalue, eigenvector pair of a square matrix **A** if they satisfy the equation

$$Av = \lambda v$$

The equation means that the vector v is special with respect to the matrix **A**. Multiplying the vector with the matrix does not change the direction or orientation of the vector. Its magnitude, however, is multiplied by the scalar λ. A square $n \times n$ matrix may have n eigenvalues $\lambda_1, \lambda_2, ..., \lambda_n$ and n corresponding eigenvectors $v_1, v_2, ..., v_n$
Therefore

$$Av_1 = \lambda_1 v_1$$
$$Av_2 = \lambda_2 v_2$$
$$\vdots$$
$$Av_n = \lambda v_n$$

Let us write this in matrix form. We construct a diagonal matrix **D** with the eigenvalues forming the diagonal and a matrix **U** with each column corresponding to an eigenvectors. Then

$$\mathbf{AU} = \mathbf{UD}$$

or

$$\mathbf{A} = \mathbf{UDU}^{-1}$$

Note that we now have the matrix **A** in terms of its eigenvalues and eigenvectors. This is the eigenvalue decomposition of **A**. The covariance matrix **F** has special properties, and in that case

$$\mathbf{U}^{-1} = \mathbf{U}^T$$

and

$$\mathbf{F} = \mathbf{UDU}^T$$

CHAPTER **7**

Testing For Tradability

INTRODUCTION

In Chapter 6 we discussed the process of choosing potential stock pairs. In this chapter we will focus on whether the identified candidate pairs are actually tradable. Based on the discussions so far, we can state that a pair is tradable if the stocks making up the pair are cointegrated. We need to bear in mind, however, that in most cases we are dealing with systems that are not exactly cointegrated. As a matter of fact, in the course of examining the candidate pairs, we can almost always expect to have a residual factor exposure causing the phenomenon of mean drift, thereby resulting in the signal to be nonstationary. However, if the signal-to-noise ratio is good enough, then for all practical purposes we could treat the residual series as stationary for the time period of the trade. Based on the preceding observations we could refine the phrasing of our question as follows: How do we decide that a pair is tradable even though it deviates from ideal conditions of cointegration? To seek out an approach to answer that, we could draw on the insights gleaned from cointegration testing procedures. With that in mind, let us outline the process of verifying that two stocks are indeed cointegrated.

Most verification processes are based on the "If it walks like a duck and quacks like a duck, it must be a duck" philosophy. Needless to add, the approach to cointegration testing is also along the same lines. We identify the properties that must be satisfied if cointegration were indeed true and check to see if the properties hold. If they do, then the stock pair in question is declared cointegrated. Let us therefore review some properties of cointegrated systems that could be potentially of use in the testing process.

We start off with the Stock-Watson characterization of cointegrated systems. Each individual stock series is modeled as a sum of a trend component and a stationary component. The property characteristic of cointegrated systems is that the trend components of the two stocks must be the same. If the trend component is the same and the stationary component just oscillates about some value, then there must be a strong correlation between the two stock series (not to be confused with the correlation between the first differences or returns of the series). A strong correlation is usually evidenced by a good fit in the regression of one time series against the other. Additionally, a good fit is characterized by a strong t statistic and r-squared measure. Therefore, deducing from the preceding information, we could look for a good value for the t statistic and the r-squared measure from the regression of the two time series, infer a strong correlation between the two series, and declare the existence of a common trend. This sounds logical, does it not? However, it is not true. Let us see why that is.

Upon careful examination of the preceding argument, it can be seen that it is actually incomplete. The argument would be complete if we could assert that the good fit upon regression or strong correlation property is a trait exclusive to cointegrated systems. Only if that were true could we conclude that evidence of the property implies cointegration. Unfortunately for us, the good fit on regression property is not exclusive to cointegrated systems. As a matter of fact and rather surprisingly, completely independent random walks when regressed against each other can also result in a high r-squared measure. This rather counterintuitive phenomenon was reported in the findings of a simulation experiment conducted by Granger and Newbold, who aptly coined the phrase "spurious regression" to describe it. Thus, as evidenced by spurious regression, the strong correlation property is not exclusive to cointegrated systems and therefore cannot be used as a definitive test for cointegration.

We now turn to another property of cointegrated systems. This is the existence of a linear combination of two time series that is stationary and mean reverting. That property is in fact a defining property of cointegration systems. We could therefore design a cointegration test based on the verification of this property. Such a test for cointegration was first prescribed by Engle and Granger. The rationale behind the test proceeds somewhat like this: If two time series are cointegrated, then a simple regression of one time series against the other should produce a good estimate of the linear relationship. Also, the spread series resulting from the linear relationship, that is, the residual series from the regression, must be stationary. Therefore, to test for cointegration all we need to do is estimate the linear relationship between the two series given using simple regression and test for stationarity of the residuals. If the residuals form a stationary time series, then we have a cointegrated pair. Thus, cointegration testing is a two-step process:[1]

1. Determination of the linear relationship.
2. Stationarity testing on the residuals.

---

[1]There is a one-step test for cointegration originally proposed by Johannsen, which I do not discuss here. However, references for it are in the appendix.

We now go back to our original question. Knowing that we are dealing with systems that are not exactly cointegrated, how do we adapt the cointegration test to test for tradability? With regard to the first step, there is not much of a change because in any case we would want to know the linear relationship between the two stocks. The difference, however, is in the second step. Contrary to the strict requirement of stationarity of the residual series for cointegration, the pair is deemed tradable as long as the residual exhibits a sufficient degree of mean reversion. I will seek to quantify this idea of mean reversion and show how the results may be used to directly verify whether a stock pair is tradable or not. Thus, similar to the cointegration testing, testing for tradability is also a two-step process: estimation of the linear relationship and measuring the degree of mean reversion. We will discuss these two steps in detail in the following section, on the linear relationship. Let us start with the estimation of the linear relationship.

THE LINEAR RELATIONSHIP

The linear relationship between the two time series is given as

$$\log\left(p_t^A\right) - \gamma \log\left(p_t^B\right) = \mu + \varepsilon_t \qquad (7.1)$$

In Equation 7.1, the left-hand side of the equation represents a linear combination of the two time series; γ in the equation is the cointegration coefficient. The right-hand side of the equation therefore represents the residual series and is expressed as the sum of two components: μ is the equilibrium value, and e_t is a time series with zero mean, which may be construed as the disturbance term in the equilibrium. If the series were mean reverting, then we would expect its value to oscillate about the equilibrium value. Owing to this, the linear relationship between the two series is also termed the equilibrium relationship, characterized by the two values γ and μ. It is therefore important to remind ourselves of the economic interpretation of these two values.

The interpretation of γ as the common factor beta between the two stocks was already discussed in Chapter 6. We are now left with the interpretation of μ. To do that, let us consider a portfolio long one share of stock A and short γ shares of stock B. The γ shares of B represents a position in terms of stock B that is equivalent to one share of A. Now, according to the equilibrium relationship, such a portfolio yields an average cash flow of μ, which is given back when the position is reversed. Thus μ represents the premium paid for holding stock A over an equivalent position of stock B. But do such premiums exist in real life? As a matter of fact, stocks do trade at a premium for a variety of reasons. Greater relative liquidity (liquidity premium), the possibility of the firm being a takeover target (takeover premium), and pure charisma on the part of some stocks are some reasons that come to mind. Therefore, in the evaluation of the equilibrium relationship care must be taken to estimate both the values γ the cointegration coefficient and μ the premium.

We will discuss two approaches to estimating the equilibrium relationship. The first approach is based on the multifactor framework. The second approach is the regression approach. Let us begin with the multifactor approach.

ESTIMATING THE LINEAR RELATIONSHIP: THE MULTIFACTOR APPROACH

In Chapter 6 we mentioned that the cointegration coefficient could be estimated by performing a regression of the common factor returns of one stock against the other. The estimated value from the regression is the cointegration coefficient. Also, the formula for the regression coefficient can be expressed in terms of the covariance and variance of the stocks involved. Now, exploiting the multifactor framework the variance and covariance may be expressed in terms of the factor exposures and the factor covariance matrix. Thus, the regression formula may be expressed completely in terms of the constructs of the multifactor framework and may be used to evaluate the cointegration coefficient.

It is important to note here that we have two values for the cointegration coefficient depending on the choice of the independent variable. If the linear relationship is expressed assuming stock B to be the independent variable, we have

$$res_t = \log\left(p_t^A\right) - \gamma \log\left(p_t^B\right) \tag{7.2}$$

$$\gamma = \beta_{AB} = \frac{\mathrm{cov}\left(r_A, r_B\right)}{\mathrm{var}\left(r_B\right)} = \frac{e_A^T F e_B}{e_B^T F e_B} \tag{7.3}$$

Alternately, if the equilibrium relationship is represented assuming stock A to be the independent variable, we have

$$res_t = \log\left(p_t^B\right) - \gamma' \log\left(p_t^A\right), \tag{7.4}$$

$$\gamma' = \beta_{BA} = \frac{\text{cov}(r_A, r_B)}{\text{var}(r_A)} = \frac{e_B^T F e_A}{e_A^T F e_A} \qquad (7.5)$$

We now have two relationships and two values for the cointegration coefficient, bringing us to the question of which value to use in our tests. We suggest going with the larger of the two. From a purely numerical viewpoint in terms of reducing precision errors, we are better off estimating the larger of the two numbers. This choice has some additional implications. To see that, let us suppose that our choice was γ (stock B is the independent variable) because $\gamma > \gamma'$, then it follows from the formulas that $\text{var}(r_B) < \text{var}(r_A)$. Thus, by choosing the larger of the two values for the cointegration coefficient, we are by implication designating the stock with lower volatility as the independent variable.

Once the value of the cointegration coefficient is determined, we can very easily evaluate the residual time series. From the earlier discussion on the linear relationship, the equilibrium value μ is the mean value of the residual time series. If this is significantly different from zero, we have a nonzero equilibrium value. Otherwise, we could assume that it is zero. To summarize, the steps involved in estimating the equilibrium relationship are as follows:

1. Calculate the two values γ and γ' using multifactor model constructs.
2. Determine which value must be used for the cointegration coefficient. Our choice is guided by the larger of the two values γ and γ'.
3. Construct the time series corresponding to the appropriate linear combination and evaluate its mean. If it is significant, we have a nonzero equilibrium value; otherwise, it is zero.

ESTIMATING THE LINEAR RELATIONSHIP: THE REGRESSION APPROACH

The linear relationship may also be estimated using a regression approach. The use of regression to estimate the linear relationship is based on the premise that if two series are cointegrated, then a simple regression of one time series against the other should give us the cointegration coefficient and the value of the premium. The slope of the regression line is the cointegration coefficient, and the intercept is the premium.

The attractiveness of the regression approach is that the general methodology of regression is well known and has found ready application in innumerable situations. Implementations of the ordinary least squares approach is part of most software packages and may be readily used on the prepared data set. In fact, it has often been argued that the simplicity of the regression process is probably its most powerful feature. Then why do we even attempt to discuss it at length? Well, it is also true that although the general idea of regression is relatively simple, the simplicity of the process lends itself to hasty application without much thought. Thus, ironically, the pervasiveness and simplicity of the regression approach is the reason to discuss aspects of the regression approach in some detail.

Proper use of regression is possible only if we thoroughly understand the standard regression scenario and the deviations of our situation from the standard. Let us therefore examine the standard regression scenario as applied to physical systems. Central to physical systems is the study of cause and effect; that is, the response of the system to a particular stimulus. If the expectation is that the response is proportional to the stimulus, the process of linear regression comes in very handy in measuring this constant of proportionality. The typical experiment involves subjecting the system to a series of inputs or a stimulus in a specified range and measuring the response of the system to those inputs. The input–output pairs then form the data set on which the regression is run. The independent variable in this case is the input or stimulus, and the slope of the regression is the constant of proportionality connecting the stimulus to the response.

Let us now highlight some aspects of the experimental process. Note that in this case, since the experimenter is the one administering the stimulus to the system, he or she can design it to be accurate with a very small magnitude of error. We can therefore assume that there is no error in the input data. However, the output data come from the response of the system and may not be known accurately due to imperfect experimental conditions. Also, if the experimental conditions do not change dramatically during the course of the trials, we may assume that the error manifest in each observation of the response is drawn from a common probability distribution. Thus, here is a situation where the input is known relatively accurately, and the source of error is only in the output with an error standard deviation that is constant across all observations.

Now let us see how stock price data relates to the scenario described above. First, it may be argued that the price of a stock is known exactly. Then where is the source of error? Note that we use just one representative value for the price in a given time period, while in actuality the price changes constantly within the period itself. Therefore, a reasonable case may be made for the existence of uncertainty or error associated with our choice for the price in the time period. Next, in our situation, there is no distinct separation of cause and effect. The prices of the two stocks may very well be feeding off each other, as discussed in the error correction model for cointegration in Chapter 5. Since it is not possible to easily separate cause from effect in this scenario, and both of the price values are read as outputs, we are now faced with a situation where there could be uncertainty or error in both variables. This is vastly different from the standard linear regression case, which assumes errors only in one variable.

Also mentioned earlier, each stock moves constantly, reaching its own highs and lows within a time period, with the high and low price characterizing the range of price movement. Although we allow ourselves to choose only one representative price for a given time period for each stock within this range, we also admit that there is a certain amount of uncertainty associated with our choice. But data points in each time period are chosen from the price ranges of different magnitudes. Under such circumstances, it would be rather facetious to assume a constant probability distribution for the uncertainty or errors that are intricately linked to the magnitude of the price range in a given period. We can strongly assert that our situation is one where the uncertainty associated with each data point is different. This is also different from the standard regression scenario of constant variance in the observations.

Therefore, to sum up, we have a situation where there is error associated with both observations, and the variance of the observation error is also a varying quantity. Although the differences of our situation with the standard regression scenario are substantial, they are by no means novel. Such situations have been encountered in a variety of other applications and may be applied to ours without change. Going that route, however, adds to the complexity of the process. We will briefly discuss the solution approach in this case to highlight the issues and proceed to suggest a much simpler approach.

The situation of nonconstant error distributions coupled with errors in both variables can be handled by minimizing the chi-squared merit function, given as

$$\chi^2(\gamma, \mu) = \sum_{t=1}^{N} \frac{[\log(p_t^A) - \gamma \log(p_t^B) - \mu]^2}{\text{var}(\varepsilon_t^A) + \gamma^2 \, \text{var}(\varepsilon_t^B)} \qquad (7.6)$$

In Equation 7.6, $\text{var}(\varepsilon_t^A)$ and $\text{var}(\varepsilon_t^B)$ are the variances of the error in the observations $\log(p_t^A)$ and $\log(p_t^B)$. The errors are assumed to have a zero mean and may be calibrated based on the range of movement of the stock within each time period. Note that for our purposes it is not important to have an absolute measure of the variance of the errors, just that the values be proportional to the actual variances.

To further understand how the chi-squared function handles the situation of nonconstant error distributions, let us examine it in a little bit of detail. The value in the numerator of the merit function is the squared error in the regression. If the variance as shown in the denominator was a constant, then the minimization boils down to minimizing the sum of squared errors, which is the ordinary least squares procedure. The denominator term, in fact, weights each data point in the cost function to be inversely proportional to the variance of the individual error terms. Thus, it may also be thought of as the sum of squared errors each normalized by its variance. This approach to regression using the chi-squared merit function is sometimes also called the weighted least squares approach.

However, typical applications adopting a weighted least squares approach assume the error only in the response variable and not in both. Specifically, those applications do not have the term with γ^2 in the denominator. The presence of this term in the denominator complicates the minimization of the chi-squared function, in that the derivative of the chi-squared function with respect to γ is now nonlinear, and so we may need to resort to numerical methods to solve this. In summary, the regression process can get fairly involved if we are to account for the varying error probability distributions in the measurement with errors in measurement for both the variables.

Nevertheless, if there is a way to construct a price series such that the errors associated with the observation in each time period may be assumed to be the same, then we can do away with these complications, work with just ordinary least squares, and arrive at a reasonable answer. Let us see if we might be able to do that.

Note that in the previous paragraph we mentioned that we choose only one representative price for a given time period from the range of stock price movement for that period. In a typical scenario where the length of a period is one trading day, the standard convention in the construction of daily time series is to use the closing price at the end of the trading day; that is, the latest price in the process of serial price adjustment. Let us call this method for recording the price time series the *close-close* method. Time series of this type are usually constructed to perform a mark to market of stock inventory. Given the nature of the auction process and the price discovery mechanism, this is definitely a reasonable choice. But is this approach to data construction appropriate for our purposes? It is seductive by habit to use the same construction regardless of purpose even though such an exercise may be ill-advised. Care must be taken to ensure that the process of data construction is a reflection of the specific purpose at hand.

Our purpose is to examine the price relationship between two stocks. In this quest, to examine price relationships, more important than the closing price in a given time period is the answer to the question, "At what price in the time period was the liquidity a maximum?" That would be the consensus price in the time chunk at which the most buyers and sellers agreed that the price was right and a lot of shares changed hands. Therefore, conclusions drawn on the maximum liquidity price series of two stocks would be more reliable than using the close-close approach. A reasonable proxy for the maximum liquidity price is the volume weighted average price, commonly termed as the VWAP price. We could therefore construct our time series with VWAP prices.

By choosing the VWAP price we are arguably within reason to assume that the error distributions of the VWAP price from the maximum liquidity price is about the same regardless of the magnitude of the price range. We can therefore resort to the simple ordinary least squares version in our regression analysis. Of course, the manner in which the calculation of standard error forming the basis for the t statistics tests would still need alteration. In our scenario of cointegration or tradability testing, the emphasis on the t statistic is rather low, and therefore we contend that this is something we can live with. Additionally, note that using the VWAP price has the tendency to temper extreme values and therefore has the added benefit of minimizing the effect of outliers on the regressions. In conclusion, the time series constructed with the VWAP price is better suited to understand equilibrium relationships and should be the preferred approach.

However, this does not do away with the need to decide which of the two price series we should use for the independent variable. We will avoid being repetitive and just say that the same idea as was adopted in the multifactor model case may be applied here, also.

TESTING RESIDUAL FOR TRADABILITY

Subsequent to estimating the equilibrium relationship we need to construct the residual time series. Although we advocated using VWAP prices to estimate the equilibrium relationship, we recommend constructing the residual time series by applying the equilibrium relationship to the time series of stocks constructed using the close-close method. If the two series are indeed cointegrated, constructing such a time series provides us with a fairly good picture of the oscillations about the equilibrium value.

We begin by reviewing the ideal situation. In an ideal situation for tradability, the two stocks would be cointegrated, and the residual series would be stationary. It is therefore desirable that the properties of the residual series exhibit the characteristics of stationary series. One of the properties of stationary series, the property of mean reversion, is of particular importance to us. This is relevant because pairs trading is a bet that the residual series will revert to its mean or equilibrium value. In other words, deviations from the mean are quickly corrected by the series moving back toward the mean. It would therefore be nice if we could quantify the degree of mean reversion of a given time series.

It turns out that highly mean-reverting series are also characterized by a high frequency of zero-crossings. A *zero-crossing* is defined as the transition of the time series across its long-run mean. The frequency of zero-crossing is then the number of times we can expect the time series to cross its equilibrium value in unit time. Thus, the zero-crossing frequency provides us with a quantitative characterization for the mean reversion property.

Notice that if the zero-crossing rate is very high, then the time to revert to mean is short, implying that the time we need to hold the paired position is small. The signal-to-noise ratio is bound to be good, and we could be more comfortable with the idea that the pair is tradable. Thus, a high zero-crossing rate for the residual series is a preferred trait and directly appeals to our requirements.

A high zero-crossing rate is also indicative of a stationary series. To strengthen this conviction, we make an observation in contrast by considering the example of Brownian motion a nonstationary series. Even though the distribution of Brownian motion is symmetric about the mean, the zero-crossing event is very infrequent. The theoretical explanation for the phenomenon is well captured by the famous arcsine law for Brownian motion discovered by P. Levy. The law provides us with information on the *last passage time*, or the last time that the Brownian motion visited zero. More precisely, let us consider a Brownian motion starting at zero, or time $t = 0$ and stopped at time T. If g is the last time when zero is visited, then the probability distribution satisfies

$$P\left(g < u\right) = \frac{2}{\pi} \arcsin \sqrt{\frac{u}{T}} \qquad (7.7)$$

The density function corresponding to this is given as

$$P\left(u\right) = \frac{1}{\pi} \frac{1}{\sqrt{u\left(T - u\right)}} \qquad (7.8)$$

A quick plot of the density graph in Figure 7.1 shows that we expect the zero crossing to have occurred with high probability only at the extremes of the time interval. Thus, we would expect very few zero crossings for Brownian motion a nonstationary time series.

For a stationary ARMA time series with known parameters, the theoretical zero-crossing rate may be calculated using the formula developed by Rice. The Rice formula is the sum of a series of zero-crossing probabilities at various time steps. The probability at each lag is calculated using the autocorrelation function. Thus, if the residual series is stationary and the ARMA parameters are known, we can apply Rice's formula to obtain the zero-crossing rate. Note that this requires us to estimate the ARMA parameters with the assumption that the series is actually stationary. This is something we wish to avoid. We favor a model free approach and will focus on that to obtain an estimate of the zero-crossing rate. Therefore, even though it would

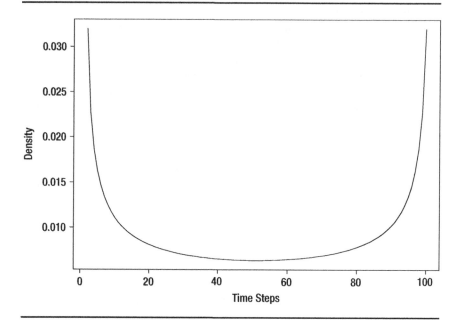

FIGURE 7.1   Density Plot of ArcSin Distribution.

be a worthwhile endeavor, we do not discuss Rice's formula in detail. Interested readers can find more specifics on this in the references at the end of the chapter.

As mentioned earlier, our focus remains on the estimation of the zero crossing rate directly from the given data sample. Obviously, the most direct approach would be to count the number of zero crossings of the residual series and calculate the zero-crossing rate by dividing the number of crossings by the total time. However, given that we are doing this with a sample size of 1, the result is likely to be strongly biased to the residual series at hand. The dilemma facing us is that we have only one realization of the residual series. The general idea of averaging across many sample residual series to rid ourselves of the bias is not possible.

To resolve this, we resort to a resampling technique popularly known as the *bootstrap*. In the bootstrap, however, we look to estimate the distribution of the time between two crossings; that is, the reciprocal of the crossing rate. Note that the time between zero crossings is directly related to the time that we expect to hold the paired position. Thus, the test for tradability also leads us to an estimate of the holding period, which can be used as a benchmark for time-based stops. The time between two crossings relates directly to the trading horizon and is therefore of direct relevance for trading.

The process works as follows:

1. First, we get the sample small size population of time between crossings by counting the time between subsequent crossings in the residual series.
2. A probability distribution is then constructed by resampling repeatedly from the existing sample. The large sample obtained as a result of the resampling exercise is then used to construct the probability distribution.
3. Percentile levels may then be constructed for the population. We can then check to see if the rates at the desired percentile levels on either side of the median satisfy our trading requirements. If they do, then we declare the pair tradable and vice versa.

Example

We now illustrate with an example the application of the process just described. For illustrative purposes, we carefully picked two stocks from the semiconductor sector and sampled their prices as of the day's close for 90 days. Although we advocate the use of VWAP prices to do the regression, for sake of expediency we ran an ordinary least squares method on it two times, changing the independent variable. Results from the regression for the larger of the two γ values are as follows:

Equilibrium value $\qquad\qquad \mu = -0.6971$

Cointegration coefficient $\qquad \gamma = 1.0617$

R-squared from the regression is 0.7965

Figure 7.2a is a scatter plot of the log-price series of the two stocks against each other. Figure 7.2b is the residual time series. A cursory look at the

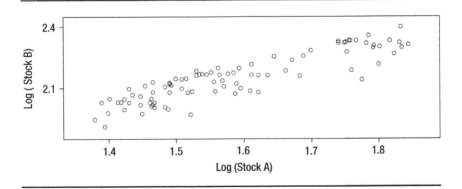

FIGURE 7.2A   Scatter Plot.

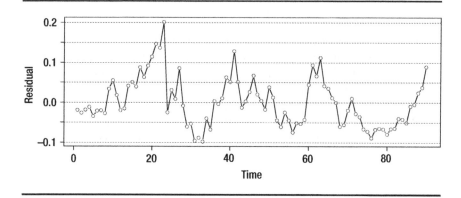

FIGURE 7.2B   Residual Time Series.

residual time series seems to suggest that it is indeed tradable. We now run the bootstrap procedure on it and obtain the population. A quick look suggests that in the extreme the time between zero crossings can be as long as 14 to 26 days with a median value of about 5 days. The pair definitely seems to be in tradable category. However, it might be better to liquidate the position on reversion to zero instead of waiting for an excursion of magnitude in the other direction.

SUMMARY

- Tradability testing is a two-step process consisting of evaluating the linear relationship and measuring the degree of mean reversion of the residual.
- The linear relationship between the log-price series of the two stocks is characterized by the cointegration coefficient and the stock premium.
- They may be estimated in a multifactor framework or by ordinary least squares regression.
- The spread series can be calculated by applying the linear relationship.
- The degree of mean reversion of a series is quantifiable in terms of the zero-crossing frequency.
- The zero-crossing frequency can be directly estimated using the bootstrap procedure.
- The reciprocal of the zero-crossing frequency is indicative of the trading period, and a pair may be deemed tradable if we are satisfied with the range of trade periods or zero crossing frequencies generated by the bootstrap.

FURTHER READING MATERIAL

Arcsine Law and Zero Crossing

Levy, P. *Processus Stochastiques et Mouvement Brownien*. Paris: Editions Jaques Gaby, 1948.
Rice, S. O. "Mathematical Analysis of Random Noise." *Bell System Technical Journal* 24 (1945): 46–156.

Linear Regression

Press, W. H., and others. *Numerical Recipes in C*, (Cambridge, UK: 2nd Edition. Cambridge University Press, 1992): 656–670.

Spurious Regression

Granger, C. W. J. and P. Newbold "Spurious Regression in Econometrics," *Journal of Econometrics* 2 (1974): 111–120.
Philips, P. C. B. "Understanding Spurious Regression in Econometrics," *Journal of Econometrics* 33 (1986): 311–340.

Resampling Methods and BootStrapping

Good, Philip I. *Resampling Methods, A Practical Guide To Data Analysis*. (Cambridge, Mass.: Birkhauser Boston, 1999).

CHAPTER 8

Trading Design

INTRODUCTION

In the discussions so far, we have established that a key requirement for pairs trading is the existence of an equilibrium relationship between the log price series of two stocks. We also discussed that the equilibrium relationship is characterized by two quantities: the cointegration coefficient and the equilibrium value. Once they are known, they can be used to construct the linear combination of the log prices of the two stocks, which is referred to as the spread. Pairs trading is a bet on the mean reversion property of the spread. When we make the determination that the spread has diverged *sufficiently* from the equilibrium value, we enter into an appropriate position in the two stocks, betting that the divergence will correct itself, and the spread would revert back to equilibrium. It is therefore important for us to explicitly define what would qualify as a sufficient divergence of the spread value from equilibrium for us to consider entering into a trade. The explicit specification of the divergence level enables us to boil down the actual trading of the spread to an unambiguous set of simple rules, which we will also refer to as trading signals. Obviously, the proper design of trading signals has a strong bearing on the profit loss picture and is therefore an important topic for discussion.

Let us look at what we would need in order to design the trading rules. Well, if the dynamics of the spread are known, then we can design our trading signals in an appropriate fashion. So, what do we know about the dynamics of spreads? For one, we can expect all of them to be highly mean reverting, since that is the criterion we used to choose the pairs in the first place. Let us assume for the sake of argument that all spreads are stationary ARMA processes. ARMA processes are mean reverting in nature and therefore do not violate the basic requirement we set forth for a pair to be tradable. So, now it is clear that the spread can at a minimum be drawn from a rich repertoire of ARMA processes and can therefore have dynamics that are wide and varied. We will discuss the different kinds of spread dynamics that we may encounter and the ramifications they hold in the process of designing trading signals.

The driving principle in the design of trading rules is the maximization of profits. The right choices could end up altering the profit picture dramatically. It is therefore important to have a robust approach to the design of trading rules. Also, as noted earlier, the dynamics of the spread have a wide and varied repertoire. Under the circumstances, it would seem most appropriate if we had different design methods for different classes of spreads, each method tailored to its class, would it not? However, that need not be the case. We propose here an approach to the design of trading rules whose main feature is its one-size-fits-all quality. The methodology may be applied to all spreads regardless of their dynamics, thus making the approach very attractive.

The game plan for the following material is to start with a simple example. We consider a white noise series and design trading rules for it. This will help to familiarize us with the underlying principles behind the design process. We follow this by discussing various classes of spread dynamics and the possible ways to model them. We then present our approach for the determination of trading signals.

BAND DESIGN FOR WHITE NOISE

Let us discuss the design of trading signals when the spread in question can be modeled as a white noise series. As noted earlier, the general principle involved in trading a spread is to put on a trade upon deviation from the equilibrium value and unwind the trade when equilibrium is restored. However, the actual implementation of the general principle could be wide and varied.

On the one hand, we can adhere closely to the general principle put on a spread position on a deviation of Δ from the equilibrium value and liquidate the position upon mean reversion. On the other hand, we could say that the spread swings equally in both directions about the equilibrium value and unwind the trade when it deviates by Δ in the opposite direction. The argument for it would be that this reduces the trading frequency by a factor of two. Given that stocks have a bid-ask spread, we would incur a trading slippage every time a trade is executed. Reducing the trading frequency reduces the effect of this slippage. The argument against it would be that this reduces the trading frequency by a factor of two and increases the holding period in the trade. This of course exposes us to mean drift, which was discussed in earlier chapters and may not be well suited to trade spreads with a lower quality of signal-to-noise ratio.

Another point to take into consideration in the trading process is the amount of inventory we are willing to hold on a spread. On one end of the spectrum, we could observe the spread at regular time intervals and put on a position whenever we spot a deviation, regardless of the current holdings in inventory relying on the statistics of the spread series to control our inventory. On the other extreme, we could limit our exposure to one spread unit;[1] that is, if we currently have one unit of spread in inventory, then even if we observe a deviation in the same direction, we do not add on to our position. However, if the spread deviates in the opposite direction, we close out our current position and enter into a new spread position in the opposite direction of our original holdings. Practical trading is probably somewhere between the two extremes.

Given the different trading styles, it would be natural to require that trading rule design be tailored to the specifics of each trading style. Fortunately for us, though, the specifics of the trading style do not matter in the determination of Δ to maximize profits. To see that more clearly, let us now walk through the process of determining the value of Δ when the spread is a Gaussian white noise series.

The Gaussian white noise series is a series of drawings from a Gaussian distribution. We buy one unit of the spread whenever we observe that the spread has a value less than or equal to $-\Delta$. Similarly, we sell one unit of the spread when we observe a value greater than or equal to Δ. The probability that a white noise process at any time instant deviates by an amount greater than or equal to Δ (Δ being positive) is determined by the integral of the Gaussian process, which is $1-N(\Delta)$. Therefore, in T time steps we can expect to have $T\big(1 - N(\Delta)\big)$ instances greater than Δ. Similarly, the probability of the value being less than or equal to $-\Delta$ is given by $N(-\Delta)$. Now, owing to the symmetry of the Gaussian process $N(-\Delta) = 1 - N(\Delta)$ and therefore the number of instances, we expect the value of the spread to be less than or equal to $-\Delta$ is also $T(1-N(\Delta))$. Thus, in a time span of T units we can expect to have bought and sold the spread on an average of $T\big(1 - N(\Delta)\big)$ times. The profit on each buy and sell is 2Δ. A measure of profitability for trading in the time period T is therefore (profit per trade × number of trades); that is, $2T\Delta\big(1 - N(\Delta)\big)$.[2] Also, note that even if we were to liquidate our positions at equilibrium value, the measure of profitability would remain the same.

Now the problem of band design boils down to determining the value of Δ that maximizes $\Delta\big(1 - N(\Delta)\big)$. Figures 8.1a and b are plots of such a function. On the x-axis is the value of Δ as measured in terms of the standard deviation of the normal density about the mean. The y-axis is a plot of the

---

[1]A unit of spread is determined by the average volume per trade in the two stocks and the ratio between them.

[2]Note that this is not the actual percentage profit as measured in conventional terms. If we do assume that we have relatively deep pockets and wish to maximize the dollar yield, then the measure as described here is appropriate.

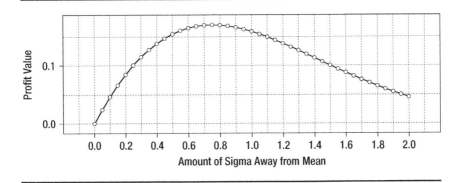

FIGURE 8.1A   White Noise Threshold Design.

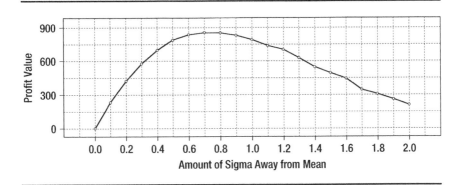

FIGURE 8.1B   Threshold Simulation with Unit Inventory Constraint.

function value. Note that the maximum occurs at 0.75σ. This would be the value that maximizes the profit.

Let us now consider the case where we restrict the inventory held at any time to one spread unit. The spread unit for our purposes is a fixed quantity of shares for the two stocks in the appropriate ratio as defined by the cointegration coefficient. Naturally, this quantity is dictated by the average trade volume of the two stocks comprising the pair.

When the spread value is more than delta and we are long one unit of spread, we sell two spread units: one to unwind the long spread position and another to have short position on the spread. The results of the analysis as already described still hold in this case. To check that this is true, we ran a simulation using 5,000 white noise realizations and calculated the profits for

different values of Δ, assuming that we trade exactly in the manner described. The plot of the profit against different values of Δ is shown is Figure 8.1b. Note that it is identical to the curve in Figure 8.1a. We can therefore safely conclude that the inventory constraints do not matter in the process of deciding the value of Δ.

Now that we understand the principles underlying the design process, it would be a good time to discuss its limitations as well. Note that there is an implicit assumption that the stocks would be uniformly liquid at all levels of divergence of the spread from equilibrium. This, of course, is far from reality. It may be that due to liquidity issues the value of delta at which the spread may be put on in size could be lesser than the one suggested by this approach. That would then be the true delta at which the profits are maximized.

This leads us to our next peeve about this approach. It says nothing at all about position size. It seems as though we could keep adding on to a pairs position and make unlimited profit when the spread converges. Needless to say, it would be naive to believe that would be the case. To see why, consider the following. By engaging in pairs trading, we are contributing to the market forces that cause the convergence of the spread. We need to make sure that at no point in time the spread position size gets to a point where we become the dominant force contributing to the convergence. If that happens, then it becomes difficult to unwind the position without a substantial slippage. Any gains we make in the spread will be lost in the slippage. It is therefore important to recognize that there is a physical limit to which we could increase the size of the pairs position, even though the design process says nothing in that regard.

So, what do we make of the design process when it does not handle these issues? A good way to look at the results of the design process is that in the absence of any information whatsoever and having to deal with making decisions in a vacuum, the results of design process serve as a strong guideline to aid in the process of designing trading rules. We now move on to some reflections on spread dynamics.

SPREAD DYNAMICS

The purpose of this section is to demonstrate that the modeling of the spread in parametric terms could indeed get complex. To get an idea of the plausible range of models for spread dynamics, we will engage in a series of what we shall call "Thought Experiments."[3] We will look at some empirical observations and the implications they bear for us when attempting to model spread dynamics. We will start with the simplest case of Gaussian white noise and reason our way toward more complicated models.

Case 1: Mixture Gaussian Model

We can expect a white noise time series for the spread to occur when trading security pairs that have a strict parity relationship. An example of this is index arbitrage, which involves trading the S&P futures against the index. But is it reasonable to expect the white noise to be strictly Gaussian? Gaussian white noise would mean the value of the spread at any point in time is drawn from a fixed Gaussian distribution. But the trading of securities is more brisk around the open and close. This causes increased volatility around these times. Hence, it would not be too much of a stretch to expect the spread series to also exhibit higher volatility around these times. We can therefore extend the white noise model by asserting that the white noise spread values are drawn from Gaussian distributions with higher standard deviations around the market open and close and a relatively low standard deviation around midday.

---

[3]A fine term coined by theoretical physicists in an era where the average physicist was expected to toil at the laboratory conducting real experiments.

In addition to that, let us now bring into consideration the empirical observation of GARCH effects in the volatility of individual stock returns. GARCH is an acronym for generalized auto-regressive conditional heteroskedascity. There is a huge body of literature on it and its ramifications for options pricing. To describe the phenomenon from a modeling perspective, let us consider a time series whose value at any point is drawn from a Gaussian distribution. If the distribution is fixed, we would have Gaussian white noise. However, we could allow for the variance of the distribution used at each point in time to vary. In fact, we go even further and prescribe that the variance of the distribution must follow an ARMA time series. If we do that, we now have a GARCH process. Although GARCH processes have been observed and recorded for individual stocks return series and not for spreads, we assert that it is definitely within the realm of plausibility that white noise spreads could exhibit the GARCH property.

In any case, to summarize the discussions so far, it seems as though it would be more realistic to model white noise spreads as values drawn from normal distributions but with standard deviations that are dependent on time. The overall distribution of the spread values in this case may be referred to as a mixture Gaussian distribution.

So, how do we design the trading rules in this case? The solution may be to resort to multiple threshold levels instead of one to maximize participation in the markets at times of both high and low volatility. We would then need to estimate the component Gaussian distributions and design the levels for each one of them. An alternate approach would be to do a dynamic estimation of the volatility using say Kalman filtering methods and let the levels vary with time.

Case 2: ARMA Model

Now let us consider the case of a stock that has just experienced a news event. We can expect the stock to trade in increased volumes with higher prices leading to higher prices or lower prices leading to lower prices, depending on the nature of the news event. In other words, we could expect stock prices to exhibit a momentum-like behavior. If this stock were to be paired up with another stock for pairs trading and the news event was specific to the particular stock, it would definitely not surprise us to see the momentum in the stock price series manifest itself as momentum in the spread series. In other words, we expect to see some correlation between consecutive values of the spread leading to a meaningful autocorrelation function and therefore an ARMA series for the spread.

So, how do we design our trading rules in this case? The underlying principles remain the same. Any choice for the threshold level has a profit per trade associated with it. If we know the rate at which the threshold level is crossed, we can determine the expected number of trades. The total expected profit is then easily calculated by multiplying the number of trades with the profit per trade. This calculation can be done for different threshold values, and the value that yields the maximum profit is chosen as the threshold.

The preceding approach necessitates that we know somehow the rate of crossing of a particular level for an ARMA series. Luckily for us, the probability or rate of zero crossing or level crossing for an ARMA process may be calculated using Rice's formula. Armed with this information, we can now say that we are ready to handle spreads modeled as ARMA processes.

Case 3: Hidden Markov ARMA Models

Recall that the ARMA series is a linear combination of past white noise realizations. Traditionally, the white noise series used in the construction of ARMA series are assumed to be Gaussian. But from our earlier discussion involving securities that enjoy a strict parity relationship, we expected the spread to be a mixture Gaussian white noise. It is therefore not much of a stretch to speculate that the underlying white noise series in the ARMA case to also be a mixture Gaussian white noise series and exhibit GARCH-like properties.

The most generalized model to cover these cases could be to say that the underlying white noise series is generated by drawing a sample from a Gaussian distribution. The Gaussian distribution is at a given time instant, however, chosen by rolling the dice. Better still, we say that the exact distribution to use is decided by a Markov process. A *Markov process* is a process where the set of outcomes of the dice rolling is dependent on the current distribution. After the distribution is decided, we then use it to draw the white noise realization. Note that the white noise generation in this case is a two-step process. The first step decides the distribution to sample from, and the second step actually draws a sample from the distribution. Models of this kind have been used in speech processing and are termed *hidden Markov models*. The parameters of such models may be evaluated using the popular Baum-Welch algorithm.

Our model construction process is not done as yet. Once the white noise process is generated using the mechanism just described, we construct an ARMA process by taking linear combinations of the past white noise realizations at each time step. (Whew!) Note that the modeling process described in this section is actually a synthesis of the models described in the two earlier sections.

So, how do we decide the threshold values in this case? As a matter of fact, at this level of complication there are no known methods as of now to evaluate the zero-crossing or level-crossing rates other than by way of simulation. One could extract the model parameters from the existing sample and generate time series data using these parameters. The profit potential of a threshold value is then estimated by simulating trades on the generated data. The profits thus calculated could then be used to determine the optimal value for the threshold.

Commentary

Reflecting on the deliberations so far, it appears that the closer we wish to model the spread to reality, the more complicated the models get. The computational methods used in these situations in turn get increasingly involved. It seems that it would be quite a formidable challenge to simplify the approach, does it not? Then again, it may be that we are not looking at the problem with the right perspective. Let us therefore restate what we wish to accomplish.

The purpose of the whole exercise is to come up with a reasonable and reliable approach to decide the threshold values. So far, the assumption has been that in order to design the threshold values it is necessary to know the dynamics of spread behavior intimately and have parametric models (models where knowledge of a few parameters gives us a complete description of the dynamics) describing their behavior. That, however, need not be the case. We would remain happy campers if we could come up with a reasonable band design without having to worry about modeling the dynamics of the spread using parametric models. So, for our purposes we resort to nonparametric methods where we estimate the profit profile function directly from the sample realization of the spread; that is, the spread series observed in the recent past. Obviously, it does not require much persuasion to subscribe to the argument that we get more of the proverbial bang for the buck on adopting the nonparametric approach.

As mentioned earlier, the idea in the nonparametric approach is to estimate the profit function directly from the sample realization of the spread. This would preclude us from having to use relatively involved computational schemes to estimate the parameters of the model had we gone the parametric route. But we have only one sample realization, and so relying completely on this realization would bias our results too much to this realization. We address this issue of bias and describe a reasonable method for threshold design in the following section, *nonparametric approach*.

NONPARAMETRIC APPROACH

One of the key issues that relate to estimating the profit function directly is the size of the spread sample. The larger the size of the sample the more confident we can be that the sample truly represents all aspects of the behavior of the spread. The statement above has in it a built-in assumption of ergodicity. *Ergodicity* has a rigorous mathematical definition and proof, but for our purposes, it may be simply stated as follows: A large sample size is effectively equivalent to having multiple realizations of the series of smaller sample sizes. Therefore, with large sample sizes for the spread, we can be reasonably confident that the effects of bias to the sample at hand have been mitigated.

However, a large sample size may be a luxury that we are not afforded. Recall that the spread dynamics are directly linked to the fundamentals of the firm and its valuation. These fundamentals are dynamic and continue to evolve with time. Therefore, the observations of the spread far back in the past may or may not be of significance, depending on whether the fundamentals of the firms involved remained more or less the same. It is therefore likely that we may find ourselves in a situation where we need to estimate the profit function from a relatively small sample data set.

We will soon describe the steps to overcome this issue and propose an approach to evaluate a close approximation to the profit function. To convince the skeptical reader that this approach actually produces reasonable results, we will apply the approach to the white noise case. We already know the true functional form of the profit in the white noise case and therefore the true optimal value for the threshold. The threshold value estimated using this approach can now be compared with the true value, thus providing us with a validation of the nonparametric approach suggested.

THE PROOF OF THE PUDDING

In the Mark Twain classic *A Connecticut Yankee in King Arthur's Court*, Merlin, the wizard in Arthur's court claims to have the ability to foresee things and know the unknown. The Yankee, pragmatic as he is, challenges Merlin to guess what he (the Yankee) is holding in his hand. As the Yankee knows what he is holding in his hand, this would serve as a ready test case to verify Merlin's claim.

In fact, the idea of the proof of the pudding is in the eating is standard fare in the area of signal processing to demonstrate the efficacy of an estimation algorithm. A sample data set for which the parameters are known is submitted to the estimation algorithm. The performance of the estimation algorithm is measured by how closely the algorithm guesses the known true value of the desired parameters. In this case, we apply the approach to the white noise case. The value obtained from the estimation can be compared with the true value to provide us some evidence of the efficacy of the approach.

We now begin the description of our approach. Note that we could choose a threshold level anywhere in the continuous range from zero to any large positive number. As a first order of business, we reduce the continuum of choices to a finite set of discrete choices for the threshold level. This is because from a trading perspective, discretization of the levels makes a lot of sense. To convince ourselves of that, let us consider the situation where we calculate the observed spread using the last traded price in both the securities. Even though the spread is calculated that way, we can typically expect to buy a security on the bid price and sell the other on the offered price. The implication is that we may have to be willing to give up the bid-ask spread in both the stocks when putting on the spread. This is called *slippage* in the process of trading. Now let us consider two candidate threshold levels that are spaced very close to each other. Note that if the spacing between them is less than slippage costs, then as far as trading goes, the two levels are virtually indistinguishable. Therefore, it does make sense to have the candidate threshold levels apart by at least the estimated slippage on trading.

Having established the candidate threshold levels that extend symmetrically above and below the mean value of the spread series, we are now ready to start the process. We begin with a simple count of the number of times the spread exceeds a particular threshold. When the threshold is above the mean, this is the number of times the spread is greater than the threshold. Similarly, when the threshold is below mean, it is the number of times it is the number of times the spread value is below the threshold. This counting method mimics the trading style where we put on a spread position whenever we observe that the threshold has been exceeded and liquidate the position when we hit the mean value. If we go with the assumption that the spread moves are symmetric about its long run mean value, we can marginally improve the estimate and reduce the bias by averaging the frequency count for the positive and negative values for the same absolute value for the threshold.

This count for each threshold level can then be multiplied by the profit value corresponding to the threshold level to obtain the raw profit function. Given that this data is from a small sample set, we can expect this to be noisy. Figure 8.2a is the plot of the probability estimates from a simple count of the number of level crossings. The underlying spread series is a white noise sample with 75 data points. Figure 8.2b is the plot of the profit made for trading the spread at a particular threshold, which is equal to the threshold value itself. Figure 8.2b is therefore a straight line with slope 1. The raw profit profile is a product of the two values for a given threshold.

Figure 8.3 is a plot of the raw profit profile for the white noise sample with 75 data points, as shown. One can see how noisy and jagged the curve is. If the raw curve were to be used as is, it could be rather confusing to arrive at any meaningful conclusion on where exactly the thresholds must be placed.

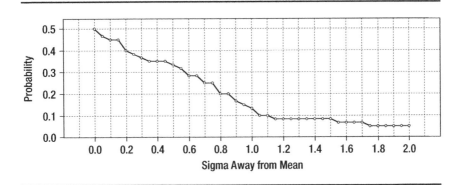

FIGURE 8.2A   Probability Estimates from Counts.

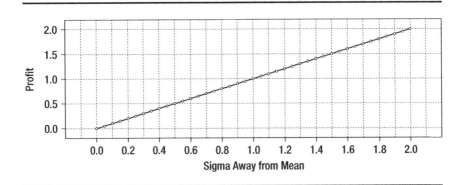

FIGURE 8.2B   Profits Levels.

Let us now attempt to explain the reason why we obtain such a noisy estimate for the profit profile. Note that we have a fine level of discretization that is coupled with a small sample size. This has led to a step function form for the count function, which in reality is expected to be monotonically decreasing. Also, notice that whenever we hit a step, the profit profile kinks upward. We shall term this the *discretization effect*. To obtain a frequency count that is monotonically decreasing, we would need to correct for this discretization effect. We can correct for the discretization effect and ensure a monotonically decreasing function by performing a simple linear interpolation between the points constituting the two levels in the step function. To show what we mean, look at Figure 8.4.

After this adjustment, even though the count is monotonically decreasing, it is still not smooth. The solution we propose to overcome this is widely

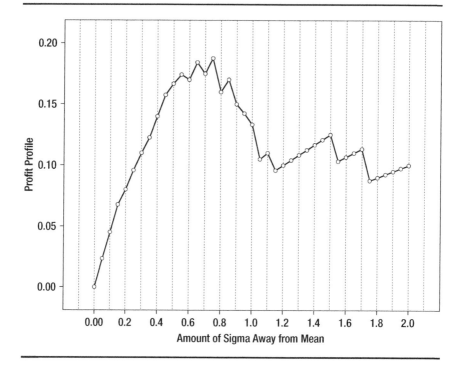

FIGURE 8.3 Profitability of Thresholds: No Inventory Constraints.

known as *regularization*. The following section contains an in-depth description of the regularization process. Upon completion of the regularization process, the resulting count function may be used to calculate the profit profile and the maximum value read off as the optimal threshold value to use.

REGULARIZATION

Let us restate the problem for sake of clarity. We are attempting to estimate the frequency function for level crossing given a sample realization. Such problems involving the estimation of functions given data fall under the general subject area of inverse problem theory. Regularization is one of the most basic ideas of this theory. The fundamental idea in regularization is that of two cost measures. The first cost measure quantifies the degree of agreement of the computed function to the given data. The second cost measure quantifies the deviation from a known property of the function like

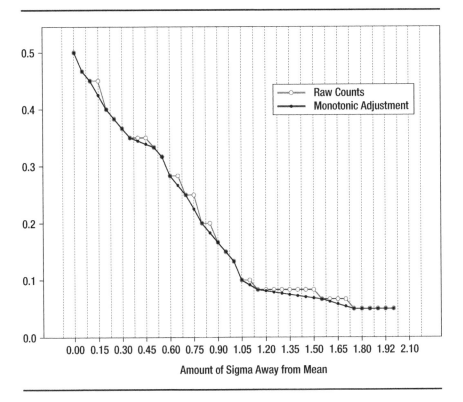

FIGURE 8.4   Raw Counts Adjusted for Monotonicity.

smoothness. In the process of evaluating the function given data, it is very likely that the two cost measures are somewhat at odds with each other. If we decide to fit the functional form very closely to the data, then we may have to give some slack on the degree of smoothness of the data. However, if we adhere strongly to the notion that the function is smooth, we may have to sacrifice on the agreement of the function to the data. The choice of the function therefore involves a delicate balancing act between the two cost measures. Note that the previously mentioned idea can also be couched in terms of the classic and ubiquitous notion in statistics of the compromise between goodness of fit and bias. If the reader is thinking that the idea has a familiar ring to it, it is probably because we visited this notion before in Chapter 2 (and you can be sure that you will read of this again in the book).

Depending on the nature of the second cost measure that relates to the property of the function being estimated, regularization is referred to by many different names. Methods that use a log-like function for the cost measure are popularly called *maximum entropy methods*, or MEM methods for short. If the cost measure is the sum of the squared difference between adjacent points in the estimated function, then it is called *Tikhonov-Miller regularization*.

So, the question now turns to what kind of regularization we should use in our case; that is, what property of the function should we try to capture in the regularizing cost measure? In addition to being monotonically decreasing, the other property that we can expect from the function is that it is smooth. We could therefore use the Tikhonov-Miller regularization to ensure smoothness of the resulting estimate. We now describe the Tikhonov-Miller process.

We are given data points $(x_1, y_1), (x_2, y_2), (x_3, y_3), \ldots, (x_n, y_n)$. The x_i series in the data set refer to the threshold values, and the y_i series are the counts corresponding to them. If this data set is representative of the actual function, then we should use the values of y as is in the final function. However, the data are from a single sample set and therefore contain the peculiarities unique to this sample, leading to a step function form for the counts. We expect the curve to be a smooth monotonic decreasing function. As mentioned earlier, we introduce a penalty term for the roughness of the curve. This penalty term is the sum of squared differences between adjacent points of the estimated function. The cost function to minimize is now a weighted sum of the two cost measures as shown next.

Let $z_1, z_2, z_3, \ldots, z_n$ represent the estimated function for the points $x_1, x_2, x_3, \ldots, x_n$ correspondingly. The cost function with the two terms is then

$$
\begin{aligned}
\text{cost} = \left(y_1 - z_1\right)^2 + \left(y_2 - z_2\right)^2 + \ldots + \left(y_n - z_n\right)^2 + \\
\lambda\left[\left(z_1 - z_2\right)^2 + \left(z_2 - z_3\right)^2 + \ldots + \left(z_{n-1} - z_n\right)^2\right]
\end{aligned}
\tag{8.1}
$$

It is easy to recognize that the first part is a least-squared cost measure, and the second part is the penalty for roughness of the curve. Note that this cost measure is multiplied by a term λ. This is the trade-off factor, and it a measure of how much of a fit error we are willing to allow for reducing the smoothness cost by one unit. The problem of Tikhonov-Miller regularization is to minimize this function with an appropriate value of λ. Note that the choice of λ is crucial, as it determines the trade-off between smoothness and fit error and, in turn, the final shape of the function. So, how do we determine the correct value for λ and the resulting regularized function? We will describe the process by way of example.

Let us consider a simulated white noise sample that we generated. We design the threshold values and do a basic count of the number of times the spread exceeds the thresholds. The count is this example is represented as a fraction, which is obtained by dividing it by the total number of sample points. Then we construct the cost function corresponding to these counts. Strictly speaking, a constrained minimization would need to be performed on the cost function by anchoring the count fraction at zero to be at the value 0.5. This is to recognize the assumption of symmetry of the spread about its mean; that is, the total count fractions above and below the mean are likely to be at 0.5. However, we will do just the unconstrained version here.

The cost function just shown is then minimized using various values of λ to obtain estimates of the count fraction function. A plot of the fit error against values of λ in a log scale is shown in Figure 8.5. Note that the fit error remains relatively constant, close to zero for small values of λ. For these small values of λ, the fit error dominates the cost function. After a particular threshold value, further increases in λ are accompanied by fit error increases. Let us call this threshold value the heel of the curve. This is the point after which the regularization cost measure takes control. Increases in λ lead

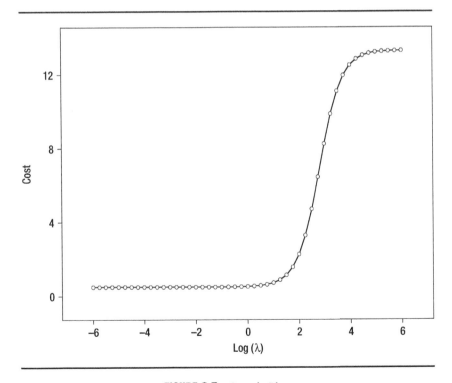

FIGURE 8.5 Lamda Plot.

to a deterioration of fit in favor of increased smoothness. Then again, past another value of λ, the fit error becomes insensitive to the λ value. At this point the function is more or less a straight line at the mean of all the points (since this is the line that would lead to the lowest cost for the smoothing function.

Our choice for λ is right at the heel of the curve. If we move λ to the left of the point, then the fit error dominates the cost function. Moving to the right of the point results in the smoothing term dominating the cost function. Choosing the value of λ to be at the heel of the curve achieves a fine balance between the two cost measures and is the value that we choose.

The function values for this value of λ are evaluated and plotted in Figure 8.6. The profit profile is then computed from the regularized curve and is as shown in Figure 8.7. The maximum is now easily read off from this graph and determines where we place the threshold for our trading signal. The maximum occurs at 0.75 times the standard deviation, which is also the theoretical value, thus validating our approach.

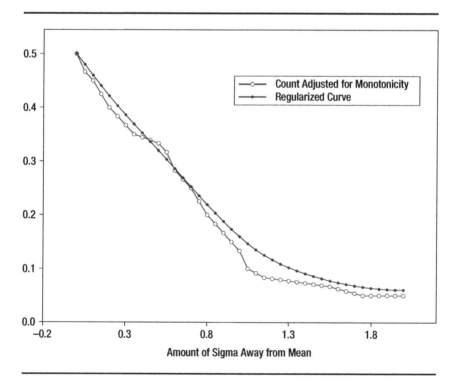

FIGURE 8.6 Regularized Plot of Counts.

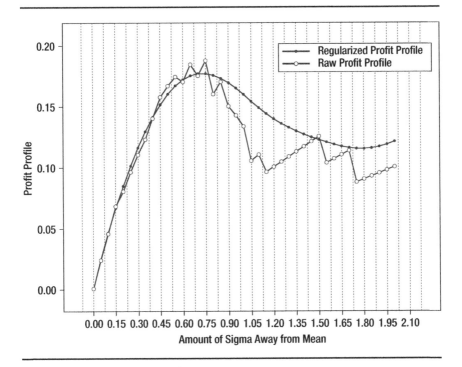

FIGURE 8.7 Profit Profile Estimation.

TYING UP LOOSE ENDS

In this section we highlight some issues of importance that were not covered in the earlier discussions.

Multiple Thresholds Design

As mentioned earlier, the need for multiple threshold design arises when the spread is generated using a mixture density white noise process. We could do this by segmenting the time series sample based on periods or time of day. The thresholds are then estimated for each sample. Subsequently, they are checked to see if the difference between the values corresponding to the data sets is significant. If it is, then we have multiple thresholds. Otherwise, we stick to the single threshold approach. Note that in the case of multiple thresholds there are inventory limits to be decided at each level, and the problem is far from being solved in a conclusive manner.

An approach to circumvent multiple threshold design is to do the threshold estimation in a dynamic fashion. The levels to apply currently are determined based on the data in the immediate past. The process could be repeated at regular time intervals and the spread levels determined on a continuous basis.

Sharpe Ratio Calculations

We will desist from calculating the Sharpe ratio for a single pair because the portfolio of pairs traded determines in a great way the eventual Sharpe ratio.

Time-Based Stops

As noted in Chapter 6, the mere passage of time adds to the risk of holding an unconverged spread. This is because of the residual common factor exposure resulting in the phenomenon of mean drift. With the passage of time, the SNR ratio deteriorates. We therefore need to calibrate the SNR ratio at which we would end up unwinding the position regardless of convergence.

In some cases it may be worthwhile looking at unwinding at the mean value or zero spread instead of waiting for the spread to swing to the opposite direction.

SUMMARY

- When trading the spread, it is desirable to trade at threshold levels that yield the maximum profits.
- A large threshold value trades infrequently for a large profit, and a small threshold value trades frequently for a small profit.
- The optimal value for the threshold is between the extremes.
- Finding the optimal value for the threshold is easier done using non-parametric methods rather than parametric methods.
- The profit function to be maximized can be constructed from sample data using a two-step process of ensuring monotonicity of the crossover distribution followed by Tikhonov-Miller regularization.
- The abcissa for the maximum value of the profit function is the desired threshold value.

FURTHER READING MATERIAL

Hidden Markov Models

MacDonald, Iain L., W. Zuchinni and W. Zucchii. *Hidden Markov and other Models for Discrete Valued Time Series.* (Boca Raton, Florida: CRC Press, 1997).

Ergodic Theory

Walters, Peter. *An Introduction to Ergodic Theory.* (New York: Springer Verlag, 2000).

Three

Risk Arbitrage Pairs

CHAPTER 9

Risk Arbitrage Mechanics

INTRODUCTION

Risk arbitrage in its general connotation relates to trading around corporate events that alter the capital structure of a firm. Note that we have introduced two terms, *capital structure* and *corporate events*. Let us briefly describe what they mean, starting with capital structure. When a business wants to raise initial capital to finance its operation, it can generally do it two ways. One way is to borrow money from lenders and pay interest on the borrowed capital. This approach is also called *issuing bonds* or *issuing debt*. The other approach is to promise a percentage ownership in the business commensurate with the fraction of capital invested. This is known as *issuing equity*. A firm may choose to go entirely one route or alternately issue equity for some portion of the capital and issue debt for the remainder. The percentage of debt and equity that comprise the firm's capital is termed *capital structure*. It is important to note that the study of capital structure and its impact on firm value is a vast subject area in itself. However, for our purpose, the simplistic definition will suffice. We now move on to Corporate event. A *corporate event* may be described as an action undertaken by a company that affects its shareholders and/or bondholders. Typical corporate events could be paying of dividends, stock splits, tender offers, mergers, exchange offers, spinoffs, and recapitalizations. Of these events, the paying of dividends and stock splits do not affect capital structure. The others, however, could potentially alter the capital structure of the firm. So, in the context of risk arbitrage we are interested only in those.

Let us briefly describe each of the corporate events of interest. Recapitalizations are situations in which companies deliberately decide to alter their capital structure. The current shareholders or bondholders would receive securities or a combination of cash and new securities in exchange for their shares. Spinoffs occur when a firm splits its business into separate units. Current shareholders receive new shares in the spun-off entity in addition to the current shares owned by them. A tender offer is a situation that occurs when a company decides to acquire another company. Shareholders of the acquired company receive cash in exchange for their shares. In exchange offers and mergers, shareholders of the acquired company receive shares in the acquiring company in exchange for their shares. Sometimes, in the case of mergers and tender offers, the acquired company shares are exchanged for a combination of cash and shares. In all of these situations the commonality lies in the fact that they involve an exchange of one security for another on a scheduled date in the future. Trading on the price disparity between the two exchanged securities is termed *risk arbitrage*.

How does pairs trading figure in all of this? The answer is quite straightforward. Of the two securities involved in the exchange, we buy the lower-priced security, sell the higher-priced security, and lock in the price difference for our profit. Note that this is possible only when both the securities in question are traded currently in the open market. In the case of recapitalizations and spinoffs, one side of the exchanged securities is issued afresh and cannot be traded before issue. Keeping with the theme of pairs trading, we therefore focus on mergers and exchange offers.[1]

HISTORY

Risk arbitrage in America is more than 100 years old. In the 1890s, there was a five-year depression and about one quarter of the railroad industry faced bankruptcy and was reorganized. In the reorganization, old debt was exchanged for new debt plus equity consisting of both preferred and common stock. The new securities often represented more value than the old ones. As a result, arbitrageurs could buy the debt and sell the new securities after a time for a profit.

Another occasion conducive for the practice of risk arbitrage was when the large processing industry trusts were converted to corporations. Trusts were vehicles for interstate commercial activity when holding companies were not permitted by state law. Subsequently, the New Jersey Holding Company Act permitted the trusts to be reorganized. In these reorganizations, arbitrageurs could buy trust certificates in the market and exchange them for new preferred and common stock that the market bid at a pre-

---

[1]Quite a large percentage of risk arbitrage practitioners focus primarily on mergers and acquisitions. Some of the practitioners trading around recapitalizations and bankruptcies call their practice distressed security investing, or, more colorfully, as vulture investing. It is also true that the two differ significantly in their method of security analysis, not to mention the even greater difference in the legal aspects surrounding them. We are thus here in this murky area of nomenclature, and what exactly falls under the umbrella of risk arbitrage could be debated.

mium. For Bernard Baruch and other players of the day, this presented a good arbitrage opportunity.

America experienced its first merger boom in the early 1900s. Shares of one company could be exchanged for shares of another for the first time. There were plenty of deals. Subsequent merger booms occurred in the 1920s, 1960s, 1980s, and late 1990s. Risk arbitrage was practiced in some form or another during these periods with the arbitrageurs acting as market makers for investors.

The practice of risk arbitrage in its modern form probably started a little after World War II. In the early days, it was done by an exclusive club of stock traders. Some of the individuals in the group were Gustave Levy, later senior partner at Goldman Sachs; Salim Lewis of Bear Stearns; Harry Cohn of L.F. Rothschild; Joseph Gruss of Gruss & Co; and Eugene Wyser-Pratt of Bache. The group was secretive about their trading methods, and the practice was shrouded in mystery. The trading was, however, based on publicly available information.

Then, in the mid 1980s Ivan Boesky wrote a book[2] on risk arbitrage, and a lot of the details on the practice of risk arbitrage came to be known publicly. Later, when the SEC charged him with insider trading offenses, the practice of risk arbitrage took a big hit. It took a while for the erroneous perceptions to come to terms with the fact that risk arbitrage can indeed be practiced based on information gathered from public sources. Since then, the business has rebounded and competition in the marketplace has steadily increased. There are now quite a few mutual funds and hedge funds specializing in risk arbitrage.

THE DEAL PROCESS

One of the crucial components in the practice of risk arbitrage is the understanding of the deal process. Any discussion on the subject matter without talking about the deal process would be incomplete. Let us therefore briefly outline various steps involved in a deal. The term *deal* is used generically to refer to both mergers or exchange offers. In the ensuing discussion we will highlight both the similarities and the differences between them.

The typical chain of events leading to a merger is as follows. First, the two companies do their due diligence on each other's business and sift through the nitty-gritty. The attorneys for both the companies then draft a contract known as a *definitive agreement*. The two companies then make the announcement through a joint press release. In some instances, the

---

[2]I. F. Boesky, *Merger Mania-Arbitrage: Wall Street's Best Kept Money Making Secret.* New York: Holt, Rinehart and Winston, 1985.

announcement is made prior to the drafting of the definitive agreement. In such cases, the announcement would be construed as an agreement in principle. Subsequently, a registration statement is filed with the Securities and Exchange Commission (SEC). The SEC looks at the statement in the context of various legal statutes causing rounds of amendments based on its comments. Subsequently, the registration statement is declared "effective," and the document is mailed to the shareholders for their approval. The shareholders vote then takes place and is followed by deal closing.

An exchange offer is somewhat of a hybrid between a merger and a tender offer. It is an unsolicited bid like in the case of a tender offer. However, unlike the tender offer, the bid is made in terms of the acquirer's stock as opposed to cash. Thus, in this aspect, it is similar to mergers. The formal exchange offer is made though advertisements in the *Wall Street Journal* and local newspapers. Since this involves the issuance of new stock, it goes through the same registration process with the SEC as is required for mergers. In this case, however, the completion of the transaction does not require a shareholders' vote.

Also note that mergers and exchange offers both have quite a bit in common with regards to their transaction terms. This is the topic of discussion in the next section on transaction terms and unless specifically mentioned, our discussions apply to both of them.

TRANSACTION TERMS

Transaction terms, in the case of mergers, are usually contained in the proxy statement that is part of the merger agreement document. In the case of an exchange offer, the transaction terms are available in the exchange offer advertisement.

It is useful at this point to specify the convention used in the ensuing discussion. The two companies involved in the transaction will be referred to as the bidder (B) and target (T). In all of our references involving exchange of shares, the convention we will follow is as follows. The shares of the target firm are given up and exchanged for shares of the bidder firm. With that, we are now ready to discuss transaction terms.

The valuation of the target firm during the due diligence process is typically in dollar terms, leading to a specific dollar amount for the target stock. While this dollar amount may be agreeable to both the parties involved in a transaction, note that it is a little hard to pay the exact specific dollar amount. This is because the payment for the target stock is made in terms of the bidder stock, and the price of the bidder stock varies on a day-to-day basis. Therefore, the key challenge in structuring the transaction is in finding an approach to pay a specific dollar amount for the target stock that is equitable to both the bidder and target companies.

The preceding description of the merger process may seem cut and dried. Nothing, however, could be further from the truth. The due diligence is intense, and negotiations are complex. To get an idea of the extremes to which the process can play out, we strongly suggest reading "Barbarians at the Gate: The Fall of RJR Nabisco,"[3] a narrative on the RJR Nabisco leveraged buyout.

As for the arbitrageur, the process is fraught with uncertainty (in some cases more than the others). Antitrust issues, actions of other potential bidders, second thoughts on part of the principals involved, financing problems, defensive merger tactics (poison pills), problems during the shareholder voting process, a general collapse of the overall market, and reaction of market participants to merger announcement (the laundry list goes on) are all issues that the arbitrageur needs to consider while placing the bet. In fact, the practice of risk arbitrage could require one to be a renaissance man, knowledgeable in analyzing financial statements, well versed in legal procedures, and be a trader, all at the same time.

---

[3]Brian Burrough and John Helyar, "Barbarians at the Gate: The Fall of RJR Nabisco." *HarperCollins* (Jan. 1991).

The role of the transaction terms in a deal is to mitigate some of the variability of the price of the bidder stock and try to achieve the objective of paying a specific dollar amount for the target stock. We now list typical transaction terms that one is likely to encounter.

Fixed Ratio Stock Exchange

The simplest form of a merger transaction is the stock for stock transaction. Shares of the target are exchanged for shares of the bidder in a fixed exchange ratio. This exchange ratio is determined by the accountants and analysts of the merging companies based on the valuation of the target firm. It is, however, self-evident that in such fixed exchanges the price paid for the target varies with the stock price of the bidder.

Fixed Value Stock Exchange

The fixed value stock exchange may be considered an attempt to do a better job at mitigating the variability. The transaction structure also helps to prevent excessive shorting of the bidder stock on the eve of deal announcements. In such transactions, the dollar value of the target stock is fixed. The exchange ratio is then determined based on the stock price of the bidder during what is known as the *pricing period*. A commonly used approach is to use the average closing price of the bidder stock in the pricing period to determine the exchange ratio. For example, if the price of the target stock is fixed at $10 and the average of the closing prices of the bidder stock during the pricing period is $20, then the exchange ratio is 0.5; that is, two shares of the target stock is good for one share of the bidder stock. Sometimes, to prevent manipulation of the closing price by arbitrageurs, the volume weighted average price during the pricing period is used to determine the ratio. Thus, in the fixed value approach, the exchange ratio is gradually revealed as the prices unfold over the pricing period.

Although, on a rare occasion, the average of the closing prices on a predetermined number of randomly chosen days in the pricing period has also been used to determine the exchange ratio, the typical approach is to use some sort of average. The length of a typical pricing period is 20 trading days or less. The length is fixed more or less to mitigate the effects of volatility on the bidder stock. Although this approach works slightly better than the fixed ratio approach, it is still subject to some extent on the volatility of the bidder stock.

Stock and Cash Exchange

The effect of bidder stock volatility on the exchange ratio may be further mitigated by paying for the target stock with a combination of cash and securities. Generally speaking, though, the exchange ratio in this case could be determined using either the fixed ratio or the fixed value method. We illustrate the transaction terms with an example.

Bidder B pays for target T, 70 percent in stock, 30 percent in cash. The share exchange ratio is 0.5; that is, 1/2 a share of B for one share of T. Cash amount paid for the remaining 30 percent is $20. Based on the preceding specification, let us now compute the exchange on a per target stock basis.

Share amount: share percentage × ratio = $0.7 × 0.5$ = .35

Cash amount: cash percentage × cash value = $0.3 × \$20 = \$6.0$

Thus, for each share of the target the holder of record would receive 0.35 share of the bidder and $6 in cash.

Note that while these sets of transaction terms reduce the dependence of the exchange ratio on the price of the bidder stock, paying partly in cash reduces the amount of equity issued and has an effect on the capital structure of the new entity.

Collars

An explicit attempt to reduce the dependence of the exchange ratio to the volatility of the bidder stock without resorting to cash payments can be seen in the case of collars. *Collars* are transaction terms that are contingent on the price of the bidder. They come primarily in two flavors, the fixed exchange collar and the fixed value collar.

In a fixed exchange collar, a constant exchange ratio is specified over a range of the Bidder's stock price. This ratio is subject to adjustment; that is, to a maximum or minimum value if the bidder's stock price falls out of the range. In a fixed value collar, a constant dollar value is set for each share of the target stock. The ratio is then determined using the pricing period approach. However, the terms would be adjusted to a maximum or minimum exchange ratio if the bidder's stock price falls out of the range.

Also included in some cases is a *walk away* right, which grants the target company an option to terminate the deal in case the price of the bidder falls below a specified level. In other cases, the bidder is also granted a termination option if the stock price of the target experiences a very steep increase after announcement.

THE DEAL SPREAD

The transaction terms in a merger or exchange offer create a strict parity relationship between the bidder and target stocks. Violations of this parity relationship can be measured based on the stock prices of both the stocks and is called the spread. To see how the spread is calculated, consider the fact that each target share is exchanged for a fixed number of bidder shares or bidder shares plus cash, the value of which we shall call the exchange value of a target share. This can be calculated exactly with the knowledge of the transaction terms and the current price of the bidder stock. Let us say that we also know the current price of the target stock. The spread is now given as

Spread = exchange value of a target share – current price of target share

The magnitude of the spread is indicative of the disparity and is therefore representative of the profit potential in dollar terms on a per-target share basis.

Prior to the date of deal completion, the target shares almost always trade at a discount to their exchange value. This implies that the value of the spread as calculated above is usually positive. Let us see why that is. If the spread were negative—that is, the exchange value of a target share is less than the current price of the target share—then there is not much reason to hold the target stock. One could sell the target stock right away and make more money than waiting until deal close. If the spread is zero, then also it makes no sense to wait until deal completion date, as it is better to cash in right now than wait till deal completion to get the same amount of money. In either of the cases, market participants would begin to sell the target stock until the value of the spread is no longer negative or zero. Thus, one can expect the spread to be positive.

It is also useful at this point to remind ourselves that there is the risk of deal break. Now, it is natural for market participants to expect a greater reward for greater deal break risk and a lesser reward for taking moderate risks. This is also reflected in the spread with large spreads, implying high risk and vice versa. Thus, the spread is indicative not only of the return but also the perceived risk of deal break. Naturally, it is a key market variable that the risk arbitrageur relates to.

As an illustration, let us look at a real-life merger between Intel Corporation (INTC) and Level Communications (LEVL). The deal was announced on March 4, 1999. INTC was the bidder, and LEVL was the target. The exchange ratio was 0.86; that is, every share of LEVL was exchanged for 0.86 share of INTC. The deal was completed on August 10, 1999.

Figure 9.1a is a plot of the prices of LEVL and INTC. The price of INTC is adjusted for the exchange ratio. The first set of points in Figure 9.1a is the closing price a day prior to the announcement of the merger. We can see that LEVL registers a big jump in price on the day of the announcement, narrowing the spread to about $4.26 on a close-to-close basis. In fact, it is common on the day of announcement to see bidder shares fall in price and target shares rise. As the day of deal completion approaches, the uncertainty in the deal decreases, the spread narrows and approaches zero. This can be seen in Figure 9.1b.

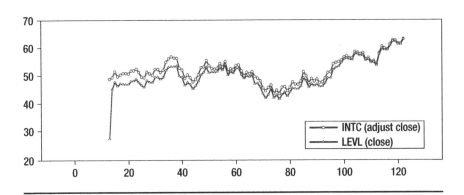

FIGURE 9.1A Price Dynamics (INTC–LEVL).

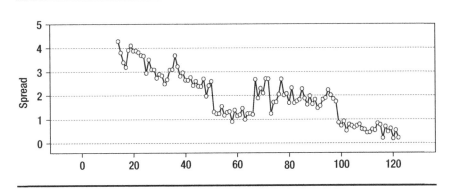

FIGURE 9.1B Spread (INTC–LEVL).

So, how do we go about trading on this disparity? This is indeed the topic for the next section, *Trading Strategy*.

TRADING STRATEGY

An arbitrageur may take on a position any time during the course of the merger process. This would, however, be dictated by the risk and return characteristics of the deal. The typical trade executed is to short the bidder shares (sell high), buy the target shares (buy low), and pocket the spread. When the deal is completed, the target shares owned are exchanged for bidder shares. These bidder shares are then applied to cover the short position.

Alternately, when it is close to deal completion (the spread is usually close to zero) the position is reversed; that is, cover short position on bidder shares and sell target shares.

In the example of INTC and LEVL, trade would be to short 0.86 share of INTC against every share of LEVL that we buy. This is done on the day of deal announcement. We would thus pocket about $4.26. When the deal is complete, the positions are reversed. This could be done in one of two ways. One way to do it is to exchange the target shares for the bidder shares and use those to close out the short position on the bidder. Alternately, we could unwind both the positions individually; that is, we sell the shares of LEVL and cover the short position on INTC. Given that the spread value around deal completion is typically zero, we can expect the proceeds from the sale of one share of LEVL would be equal to the price of 0.86 shares of INTC. These proceeds are now used to buy the shares of INTC to cover the short position. Thus, for every share of LEVL we were long, we would have pocketed about $4.26.

The following list is an example of a typical rate of return calculation for a deal.

Example

Deal Details
The spread on the deal is calculated as follows:

spread = price of B × 0.35 + 6.0 – price of T

Announcement Terms:	1/2 a share of B to be exchanged for every share of T, that is, ratio = 0.5.
Dividends:	No dividends will be paid by B or T
Current stock prices:	price(B) = $20.0, price(T) = $8.0
Spread:	$0.5 \times \text{price(B)} - \text{price(T)} = (0.5 \times 20.0) - 8.0$
	$= \$2.0$
Estimated Time to Close:	3 – 6 months. (average = 135 days)

The Strategy

1.	Purchase two shares of T	($16.0)
2.	Sell Short one share of B	$20.0
3.	Lose Dividend on B, receive dividend on T, net	$ 0.0
4.	Rebate on short position	$ 0.21
5.	Net proceeds (2 + 3 + 4)	$20.21
6.	Gross Profit (5 – 1)	$ 4.21
7.	Return = 4.21/16.0 × 165/360	12.05 %

This return is usually compared with 2×90 day treasury bill rate as the benchmark to determine if the trade is viable. Note that the return calculation here is slightly different from the return calculation used in the statistical arbitrage case. The return is calculated on the dollars invested in the long position alone. This is more to adhere to conventions followed in practice.

QUANTITATIVE ASPECTS

In the following chapters, we focus on some quantitative aspects of risk arbitrage. The focus will be in the areas of trade execution and risk measurement.

When trading spreads in size, it is not possible to trade the entire quantity in one go due to liquidity constraints. The position is therefore filled on an incremental basis. Note, however, that the trades need to be executed in what we shall call a paired transaction. We need to ensure that both legs of the pair be filled in a manner so as to satisfy the ratio constraint and also in the process manage to capture a spread that is greater than a specified value. We shall discuss issues relating to the unambiguous specification and verification of such trades.

We will then address executions in the fixed value exchange case. In the fixed value exchange transaction, we noted earlier, the exchange ratio is revealed gradually as the prices unfold during the pricing period. The exact exchange ratio is known only at the end of pricing period. However, it is possible to trade during the pricing period and still manage to be perfectly hedged. We will illustrate how trading may be done during the pricing period when the exchange ratio is unclear.

Next, we demonstrate how market implied deal break probability can be evaluated using the time series of the spread. This is followed by a discussion on how the measured probability may be applied to evaluate the value at risk in risk arbitrage deals. It turns out that the evaluation of stable estimates of the deal break probability requires us to work on a smoothed version of the spread. We delineate an approach for smoothing. The smoothing process leads us to a methodology that could be useful in timing the unwinding of the spread position.

SUMMARY

- Risk arbitrage relates to trading around corporate events, especially mergers and acquisitions.
- The practice of risk arbitrage has a long history and is a widely practiced arbitrage technique.

- The mechanics involve putting on a spread position when the deal is announced and unwinding it on deal completion.
- The spread is a key market variable that the arbitrageur relates to.
- Its value is roughly equal to the dollar profit per share of target and also indicative of the inherent risk of deal break.
- We also discuss a typical trading strategy.

FURTHER READING MATERIAL

History

Nelson, Ralph L. *Merger Movements in American History, 1895–1956.* (Princeton, New Jersey: Princeton University Press, 1959).

Nye, Richard B. and Roy C. Smith, "Event Investing" (working paper, Solomon Center, Leonard N. Stern School of Business, New York University, WP-S-95-27, 1995).

Mechanics of Risk Arbitrage & Transaction Terms

Moore, Keith M. *Risk Arbitrage: An Investor's Guide.* (New York: John Wiley & Sons, Inc., 1999).

CHAPTER 10

Trade Execution

INTRODUCTION

There is an oft-quoted maxim, "Concentrate on what you do best and delegate the rest." Going with this idea, the general preference of the arbitrageur is to concentrate on deal analysis and delegate trade execution to a broker. The execution in this case is fairly involved, as the trades need to be done on a paired basis. Not only must the broker ensure that the positions in both the stocks satisfy the particular exchange ratio, but he or she also needs to ensure that the fill prices on the stocks capture the specified spread. Thus, at all times the broker needs to ensure that the ratio and spread constraints are satisfied. Given that the execution is fairly involved, there are only a select number of brokers who accept orders to be executed on a paired basis. In any case, there is now a need to specify the order unambiguously to a broker. We will discuss the unambiguous specification of a paired transaction in this chapter. There is also a need to verify that the order was executed to satisfaction. We will also discuss issues pertaining to execution quality and the criteria that could be used to measure it.

Next, we address trade executions in fixed value exchange transactions. Recall that in such transactions, the exchange ratio is gradually revealed as the pricing period unfolds, and the exact exchange ratio is known only at the end of the pricing period. This seems to carry with it the implication that the spread position can be put on only after the end of the pricing period and not any time before that. However, that need not be the case. It is possible to put on a spread position during the pricing period and still manage to be perfectly hedged. We will discuss how that can be accomplished.

Also note that we expect to enter into a short position of considerable size on the bidder stock when putting on the spread; that is, we need to execute a short sale on the bidder stock. A short sale is the sale of stock that the seller does not own but is committed to repurchasing eventually. The New York Stock Exchange and the NASDAQ stock market require that any short sale must occur when the price is rising; that is, on an uptick. Therefore, there are fewer opportunities to execute a short sale making it relatively harder to short a stock. In fact, the uptick rule is meant to curb the impact of attempts by short sellers to drive a stock's price down through aggressive selling. We will conclude this chapter with a few remarks on short selling.

SPECIFYING THE ORDER

The first step to the successful execution of an intended trade is unambiguous specification. In the case of a single stock execution, the order must at a minimum specify clearly the ticker, the trade direction, and the trade quantity. This is essentially what is known as the *simple market order*. Additional constraints related to the price at which the trade may be executed are added to this basic instruction and specified in what is well known as *limit orders* or *stop orders*.

In the case of a paired transaction, we need to specify the bidder and target tickers, and the trade direction and trade quantity for each of them. The other constraints specified include the spread to be captured between the stocks and the ratio of the bidder to target shares. As in the case of a single order, it is also possible to get a partial fill in a paired execution. In this case, the entire specified quantity is not filled. However, the quantity of completed shares of the bidder and the target are expected to satisfy the ratio constraint, and the prices of the fills must be such that the calculated spread is greater than or less than the specified value as the case may be. Therefore, the two important constraints that distinguish a paired transaction from a single stock transaction are the ratio and spread constraints.

We discuss here the specification of the details of a paired transaction. An arbitrageur specifies an order to the broker by providing the following information.

Bidder and Target Tickers

To execute an order, we would have to know the ticker symbols of the stocks involved.

Action

This is to signal the arbitrageur's intention. The arbitrageur can either put on or unwind the spread position. Notice that this implicitly sets the direction for trading the bidder and target stocks. *Put on* implies that the broker is required to sell the bidder stock and buy the target stock. *Unwind* refers to the reversal of a spread position; that is, buy the bidder stock and sell the target stock.

Ratio and Cash Amount

The ratio and the cash amount are part of the calculation formula used to calculate the achieved spread. We repeat the formula here for convenience.

$$\text{achieved spread} = \text{price paid for bidder stock} \times \text{ratio} + \qquad (10.1)$$
$$+ \text{ cash amount} - \text{price paid for target}$$

The Spread Value

The specification of the spread value by the arbitrageur is similar to the limit order for a single stock. The broker should aim to match or beat the specified spread value. Now when the spread is put on, the arbitrageur would like for the spread to be as wide as possible. In this case, the broker should aim to achieve a spread greater than the specified value. The situation is reversed when we unwind the spread. Here, a low value for the achieved spread is good, and the broker should aim to get as low a spread as possible on the execution.

Target Stock Quantity

This piece of information in the specification is rather straightforward. Implicit in the target quantity specified is also the share quantity of the bidder stock. The bidder stock quantity may be calculated using the formula

$$\text{bidder quantity} = \text{ratio} \times \text{target stock quantity} \qquad (10.2)$$

Short Sale Indicator

The short sale indicator can take values *yes* or *no*. Putting on a spread position involves selling the bidder stock and buying the target stock. However, if we do not own any of the bidder stock already, the only way we can put on the spread is by selling the bidder stock short. Since this requires a short sale, we would expect the short sale indicator to be set to yes. Similarly, unwinding the spread involves covering the short position in the bidder with a purchase of bidder stock and selling the target stocks that we already own. This does not require a short sale, and we may expect the short sale indicator to be set to no.

In fact, we could even go so far as to say that typically, we can expect this flag to be set to yes when we put on the spread and to no when we unwind the spread. However, on occasion the arbitrageur may not have a spread position corresponding to a particular merger in his or her portfolio. Additionally, he or she may also happen to take the view that the merger is unlikely to happen and may expect the spread to diverge. To participate in such moves, the unwind order is placed first before the order to put on the spread. This is sometimes termed as *chinesing* the spread. The unwinding in these situations involves the sale of target shares without a prior position and would therefore be accompanied with a short sell indicator of *yes*.

We illustrate the order specification with an example.

Example

Bidder ticker	= HWP (Hewlett Packard Company)
Target ticker	= CPQ (Compaq Computers Corporation)
Action	= put on
Ratio	= 0.6325
Cash amount	= 0.0
Spread value	= $2.30
Target stock quantity	= 10,000
Short sell indicator	= yes

Let us see what this order means. The action is to put on the spread. That means we sell the bidder stock (Hewlett Packard) and buy the target stock (Compaq). Also, the short sell indicator is a yes. Therefore, the sale of the bidder stock (Hewlett Packard) has to be a short sale. Now that we have fixed the direction of trading for the two stocks, let us determine the specified quantities. The quantity of the target stock (Compaq) to be bought is specified as 10,000. The bidder quantity, however, is not specified. We deduce the bidder quantity from the target share quantity and the exchange ratio using the formula given. In this case, it is $10,000 \times 0.6325 = 6325$ shares. Therefore, this is an order to buy 10,000 shares of CPQ and sell short 6,325 shares of HWP. Are there any additional constraints? The answer is yes, and it is specified in terms of the spread value. The spread measured on the fill prices of the two stocks must be greater than or equal to the specified spread value of $2.30. This spread in this case may be measured using the formula

$$0.6325 \times \text{price(HWP)} + \text{cash amount} - \text{price(CPQ)} >= \$2.30$$

Thus, the order unambiguously specifies the tickers, the trade direction, trade quantity, the spread constraint, and the ratio constraint that are to be satisfied.

VERIFYING THE EXECUTION

The paired execution order as specified to the broker is usually for a considerable size in terms of the number of shares involved. Given the large position sizes and the fact that this is a paired transaction, the order is worked by the broker in a series of executions. This is done on a best-effort basis. The broker then delivers to the arbitrageur a list of executions for both the stocks. It is now up to the arbitrageur to evaluate the quality of execution.

The quality of executions may be measured two ways, speed and efficacy. In situations when there is news in the market and quick action is required, execution speed is of utmost importance and may very well be the criterion upon which the execution quality is measured. However, in most other situations the arbitrageur is interested in capturing as high a spread as possible when putting on the spread and unwinding at as low a spread as possible. In such cases, the execution efficacy, characterized by how well the executions measure up to the specified spread value, is more important. While one would ideally want to be able to capture as high a spread as possible in the shortest possible time, it is conceivable that a quick execution could mean that one gives up on efficacy, causing a trade-off between the two criteria for measurement of execution quality.

We now look at issues related to measuring execution efficacy. Of course, in the course of the discussion we will see how it affects execution speed. To measure efficacy, one can attempt to pair up the executions and check to see if each paired execution satisfies the spread constraint, how many missed the specified spread value, and by how much. A ratio of the dollar value of the hits versus the misses could very well be the measure of execution efficacy. Another option is to compare the specified spread value against the average achieved spread calculated using the execution prices of the two stocks. We could then use the difference as a measure of execution efficiency. The question therefore is, which measurement approach do we choose? We recommend going with the second method; that is, the one based on the average execution prices. We will justify our recommendation by demonstrating that the first idea of pairing up executions to judge efficacy is a process fraught with inconsistencies. To do just that, let us go through the exercise of pairing the executions. This exercise in addition to proving our point also provides insight into how we may characterize aggressive and conservative trading.

Let us start with the pairing process. The input to the pairing exercise is the list of executions. Each execution is characterized by the stock ticker, the direction of execution (long or short),[1] the fill price, and the fill quantity. The executions may therefore be partitioned into two sets based on the stock ticker. The idea is to pair the executions of one ticker against the executions of the other ticker such that the spread and ratio constraints are met. We formulate the trade pairing exercise as a network flow problem.

HISTORY

One of the important subject areas of the latter part of the twentieth century that has found successful application in a multitude of situations has been the study of network flows. The subject area was pioneered by Ford and Fulkerson. In their seminal paper published in 1956, they framed the network flow problem as an integer linear program. Besides detailing an algorithm to solve for the optimal way to route the flow across a network, they also provided a novel interpretation of the dual of the network flow linear program, now famously known as the max flow–min cut theorem.

Since then, network flows have found application in a wide variety of situations. Of relevance to finance, a subclass of the general max–flow problem, known as matching, has found application in game theory and to the theory of auctioning. Other applications of network flows range from something as practical as logistic planning to something as abstract as theorem proving,[2] making this a fascinating subject area for study in its own right.

---

[1]Since these trades are all done to fill the same order, we can expect the trade direction to be uniform across all executions for a given ticker.

[2]For an example, see Umesh Vazirani, "Rapid Mixing Markov Chains," Proceedings of the Symposia in Applied Mathematics, Vol. 44, 1991, pp. 99–121.

As a necessary preprocessing step, we evaluate the equivalent target share quantities for the fill quantities on the bidder side trades. This is accomplished by dividing the bidder fill quantities by the exchange ratio. These are the share quantities that will be used in the modeling exercise. The network flow problem can now be represented in a pictorial fashion.

Every execution is represented as a node. We pick a node from each of the two sets (bidder trades and target trades) and determine if the fill prices on the two executions satisfy the spread constraint. If satisfied, we draw an edge or line between the two nodes or executions and assign a weight or capacity to it based on the number of shares that can be matched along that edge. Thus, each edge represents a potential way to pair the executions. We wish to match as many shares of the bidder as we possibly can with the target shares. The edges and the nodes form a network called a *bipartite graph* in graph-theory parlance, and the pairing problem is equivalent to maximizing the flow on this bipartite network. The idea becomes clearer with the following example:

Example

Consider an order specification with the following data:

Exchange ratio = 1.0
Cash amount = 0.0
Spread value specified = $1.00
Action = put on

Now, since we are putting on a spread, we sell the bidder and buy the target. The spread constraint is therefore met when the calculated spread is greater than the specified value of $1. The executions list for the bidder and target stocks when putting on the spread position is listed in Table 10.1.

The pairing problem can now be posed as a max-flow problem on the network shown in Figure 10.1.

TABLE 10.1 Execution List.

	Bidder List				Target List	
Label	*Quantity*	*Fill Price*	*Ratio Adjusted Quantity*	*Label*	*Quantity*	*Fill Price*
B1	100	19.0	100	T1	50	19.0
B2	100	19.5	100	T2	150	18.5
B3	100	20.0	100	T3	150	18.0

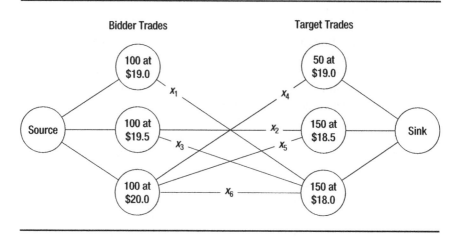

FIGURE 10.1 The Max-Flow Formulation.

Note that in Figure 10.1 we have explicitly shown the source and the sink to identify the direction of flow, which should be from the source to the sink. Each node represents an execution, and the details of the execution are listed for each node. The maximum capacity of each edge is not shown in the picture but is actually the smaller of share quantities of the nodes on either end of the edge. The pairing problem is now equivalent to maximizing the flow on this bipartite network. The linear programming formulation[3] may be written as

Maximize $x_1 + x_2 + x_3 + x_4 + x_5 + x_6$
sub:

$$x_1 \leq 100 \qquad\qquad (1)$$
$$x_2 + x_3 \leq 100 \qquad\qquad (2)$$
$$x_4 + x_5 + x_6 \leq 100 \qquad\qquad (3)$$
$$x_4 \leq 100 \qquad\qquad (4)$$
$$x_2 + x_5 \leq 150 \qquad\qquad (5)$$
$$x_1 + x_3 + x_6 \leq 150 \qquad\qquad (6)$$

---

[3]The linear programming formulation here is different from the conventional linear programming representation of the max-flow problem. The interpretation of the dual in this case is a minimum weighted set cover problem. However, since this is not germane to the discussion, we will not pursue this in detail.

$$x_1 \leq 100 \tag{7}$$
$$x_2 \leq 100 \tag{8}$$
$$x_3 \leq 100 \tag{9}$$
$$x_4 \leq 100 \tag{10}$$
$$x_5 \leq 100 \tag{11}$$
$$x_6 \leq 100 \tag{12}$$
$$x_1, x_2, \ldots, x_6 \geq 0$$

Let us examine the formulation shown here. The objective in the linear program is the sum of the flows across all the edges, and we are rightfully looking to maximize this quantity. Constraints 1–3 state that the total outflow from a bidder node must not be greater than the share quantity of that node. Likewise, constraints 4–6 ensure that the inflow into a target node must not be greater than the share quantity of the node. The constraints 7–12 fix the maximum capacity of every edge. Thus, maximizing the flow along this bipartite network leads us to a solution for our pairing problem.

The solution approach to the general max-flow problem has been well researched and a number of algorithms have been proposed to solve it. Also, the pairing problem we address has a special structure. On account of this, the solution method that would work for us is fairly straightforward. A detailed description of both the general method and one tailored to our problem can be found in the appendix. The important point, however, is that the modeling process and the solution method provide us with some insights into the nature of the pairing problem itself.

In fact, the solution approach reveals that the answer to the pairing problem is not unique, and it is possible to have a number of optimal paring configurations for a given set of executions. Looking at Figure 10.2 we can see that there are at least three possible configurations for the given set of executions in Table 10.1, begging the question as to which configuration we should use to measure execution efficiency. It is now easy to appreciate the futility of measuring efficiency by way of pairing. Note, however, that the average achieved spread is a constant value regardless of the pairing configuration. We therefore contend that it is this measure that should form the basis for verifying executions.

There is a flip side to looking at just the average spread. The broker may trade away the edge gained on an earlier execution, of course ensuring that the average spread criteria is met. To see what we mean, consider the situation with a target spread of $1.00 where the broker has completed about half of the whole order, achieving a spread of $1.05. To satisfy the average criterion, the broker needs to achieve a spread of just $0.95 on the remaining half, which may not be what was intended by the arbitrageur.

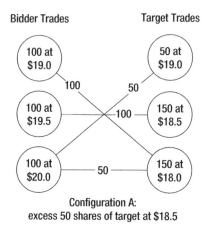

Configuration A:
excess 50 shares of target at $18.5

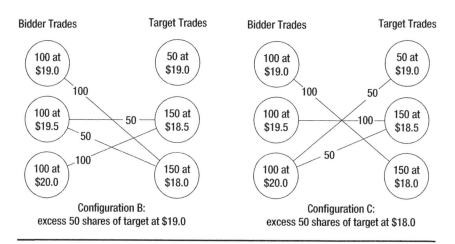

FIGURE 10.2   Redundant Matchings.

In conclusion, it would help to indicate exactly what the evaluation criterion would be to the broker. This will hopefully ensure that the execution was completed as intended. The possibilities are

1. *Conservative trading.* Ensure that there is at least one way to pair the trade list such that each pair satisfies the spread criterion.
2. *Aggressive trading.* Ensure that the average spread achieved is the same as or better than the specified spread value and therefore to the extent possible the speed of execution matters.

EXECUTION DURING THE PRICING PERIOD

In this section, we focus on trading in the context of fixed value exchange transactions. In such transactions, the exchange ratio is determined based on the stock price of the acquiring firm during the pricing period and is gradually revealed as the pricing period unfolds. Since knowledge of the exchange ratio is important to executing a paired transaction, this would imply that we can trade only at the end of the pricing period.

However, in some cases, this strict constraint may not be ideal for trading. To appreciate the fact, let us consider the situation wherein the end of the pricing period is very close to the shareholders' vote, or even worse, the end of the period is well past the shareholders' vote (these situations are not uncommon in real life). In such situations, the time interval between the end of the pricing period and the date of deal completion is rather short, leaving very little time to put on a position of substantial size. To further compound the situation, one has to deal with the prospect of rapidly narrowing spreads.

Given this, the arbitrageur would prefer to not have to wait until the end of the pricing period to put on a spread position. Therefore, even though the exchange ratio is not known exactly, the arbitrageur would want to begin trading before the end of the pricing period but trade in a way that leaves him or her perfectly hedged (meet the ratio constraints on the pair) eventually. In this section, we will discuss an approach where we trade during the pricing period and still manage to satisfy the ratio constraint at the end of the period.

Consider the case where the exchange ratio is computed on a fixed value of the target stock p^T and the average closing price of the bidder stock in the pricing period. Let the closing prices of the bidder stock be $p_1, p_2, \ldots, p_n$ starting from day 1 to day n, the last day in the pricing period. Now, according to the terms of the fixed value exchange transactions, the ratio (number of bidder stock exchanged for one target stock) is given as

$$r = \frac{np^T}{p_1 + p_2 + \ldots + p_n} \tag{10.3}$$

This is the fixed value of target stock divided by the average of the closing prices of the bidder stock in the pricing period. The reciprocal of the exchange ratio r is therefore

$$\frac{1}{r} = \frac{1}{n}\left(\frac{p_1}{p^T} + \frac{p_2}{p^T} + \ldots + \frac{p_n}{p^T}\right) \tag{10.4}$$

Interpreting Equation 10.4, the reciprocal of the exchange ratio is an average of the reciprocals of the realized exchange ratio in the pricing period. We will exploit this idea in our approach to trade during the pricing period. If we decide to put on a total spread position consisting of n^B shares of the acquirer, the number of shares of the target n^T to be bought is given as

$$n^T = \frac{n^B}{r} \tag{10.5}$$

$$n^T = \frac{n^B}{n}\left(\frac{p_1}{p^T} + \frac{p_2}{p^T} + \ldots + \frac{p_n}{p^T}\right) \tag{10.6}$$

We can write this as

$$n^T = n_1^T + n_2^T + \ldots + n_n^T \tag{10.7}$$

where

$$n_i^T = \frac{n^B p_i}{n p^T}, i = 1, \ldots, n \tag{10.8}$$

In other words, the formula tells us the amount of target shares to buy on a daily basis for a fixed number of bidder shares such that we would be fully hedged at the end of the pricing period. We can mimic this equation during execution by shorting $\frac{n_B}{n}$ shares of the acquirer and buying $\frac{n_B}{n} \times \frac{p_i}{p^T}$ shares of the target on the $(i + 1)$th day. At the end of the pricing period plus one more day, we will be perfectly hedged. Alternately, we could start by holding a naked short position on the bidder stock and buy the corresponding number of target stock on each day in the pricing period. Of course, the captured spread would vary depending on the timing of trades of the bidder stock.

There is a small caveat in all of this, though. Recall from the introductory chapter that the dollar profit is calculated on a per-target-share basis. However, the total number of target shares that we buy in this case is known only at the end of the pricing period. Thus, it would be reasonable to say that we would know our position size (in target share terms) and expected profits only at the end of the pricing period. Hence, by trading in this fashion we will have replaced our uncertainty on the ratio by the uncertainty on the position size/profits.

Example

Days in pricing period n $= 20$

Fixed value of target stock P_r $= \$60$

Closing price of bidder stock
on ith day, p_t $= \$80.5$

Total shares of bidder
to short n_B $= 100{,}000$

Shares of bidder to short for
the next day $= \dfrac{n^B}{n} = 100{,}000/20 = 5000$

Shares of target to buy for
the next day $= \dfrac{n^B}{n} \times \dfrac{p_i}{p_T} = 5000 \times (80.5/60.0) = 6708$

Bounds on the Position Size

It was noted in the last section that when trading during the pricing period, an arbitrageur has to be willing to replace the uncertainty in exchange ratio with an uncertainty in position. However, there is still an interest in evaluating some bounds on the position size of the target shares. In this section, we derive some bounds on the ratio and show how it can be converted to bounds on the position size.

To see how we can estimate bounds on the ratio, consider the fact that the average of the closing prices of the stock is always between the maximum and the minimum prices. Thus, a very simple bound could be based on that. If we assume a log-normal process for the price movement of the bidder stock, that is, the logarithm of the prices executes a Brownian motion, the probability distribution for the maximum of a Brownian motion in time t is given as

$$F_{\max} = 2\phi\left(\frac{x}{\sigma\sqrt{t}}\right) - 1, \, x \geq 0 \tag{10.9}$$

where σ in the equation is the volatility of the Brownian motion and Φ is the cumulative density function of the normal distribution. The formula represents the probability that the Brownian motion will have a maximum value less than or equal to x in the time duration t. By symmetry we can expect the distribution of the minimum to be a flipped version of distribution of the maximum for values less than 0. A plot of the distribution functions for the maximum and minimum is shown in Figure 10.3.

Reading the graph, one can say that the maximum value of the Brownian motion is less than the standardized value of 2.0 with 95-percent accuracy,

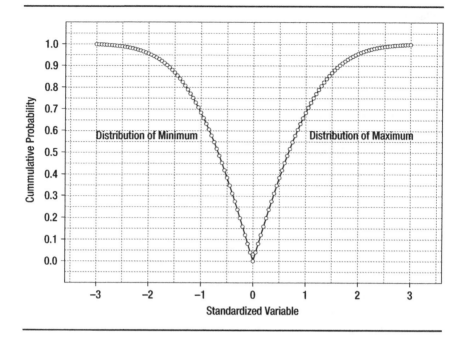

FIGURE 10.3 Distribution of the Max and Min of Brownian Motion.

the standardized value being $\dfrac{x}{\sigma\sqrt{t}}$. Thus, we can say with 95-percent confidence that the average value of the Brownian motion will be between $x = -2\sigma\sqrt{t}$ and x.

We now combine the preceding information with the fact that the mean of a sample is definitely lower than the maximum of the sample. The maximum can now be used as an upper bound for the mean. In a similar manner, the minimum serves as a lower bound for the ratio. The bounds on the ratio can quickly be translated into bounds for the target share quantity by multiplying the ratio bounds with the Bidder shares quantity. Thus, an estimate of the maximum and minimum price during the pricing period may be used to calculate the bounds on the exchange ratio.

We, however, believe that we could obtain a tighter bound than the one just shown. To see that, let us consider the average of n numbers $x_1, x_2, \ldots, x_n$. Now let the upper bounds for each of the numbers be $b_1, b_2, \ldots, b_n$. Then

$$\frac{x_1 + x_2 + \ldots + x_n}{n} \leq \frac{b_1 + b_2 + \ldots + b_n}{n} \tag{10.10}$$

Saying this in words, the upper bound for the average is the average of the upper bounds. It is easy to see that the same argument is also true for lower bounds. Exploiting this idea, we compute the bounds on the maximum and minimum for each day in the pricing period and use the average of the bounds as the bound for the average. This is illustrated in the following example.

Example

Consider the bidder stock selling at $80, 15 days into the pricing period consisting of a total of 20 days. The realized average price in the 15 days for the bidder stock is $79. The volatility of the bidder stock on an annualized basis is 32 vol. The value of a target share is fixed at $60. We plan on shorting 100,000 bidder shares. So, what are the bounds on the number of target shares that we would end up holding in the end?

Step 1: List the given information.

The daily volatility $\sigma = 32/\sqrt{252}$ $= 2.01\%$
Number of days to end of pricing period, $N = 5$ days
Current average price avg_c $= \$79$
Current closing price p_{close} $= \$80$
Total days in pricing period, T $= 20$ days
Fixed value of target stock p_{tgt} $= 60.0$
Number of bidder shares n^B $= 100{,}000$ shares

Step 2: We now compute the individual bounds in Table 10.2.

TABLE 10.2 Bounds on Size of Target Position.

Days	Scaling Value	Incremental Bound	Log of Upper Bound	Log of Lower Bound	Price Upper Bound	Price Lower Bound
n	$\sqrt{n}$	$2\sigma\sqrt{n}$	$\log(p_{close})$ $+2\sigma\sqrt{n}$	$\log(p_{close})$ $-2\sigma\sqrt{n}$	$e^{\log(\text{UpBound})}$	$e^{\log(\text{lowBound})}$
1	1.000	0.0402	4.4222	4.3418	83.2815	76.8478
2	1.414	0.0569	4.4389	4.3252	84.6798	75.5788
3	1.732	0.0696	4.4517	4.3124	85.7687	74.6192
4	2.000	0.0804	4.4624	4.3016	86.6976	73.8198
5	2.236	0.0899	4.4719	4.2921	87.5243	74.7976

Step 3: Calculations

The average price upper bound for the five days, *upperAvg* = 85.5904

The average price lower bound for the five days, *lowerAvg* = 74.7976

The final price upper bound,

$$p_{\text{upper}} = \frac{(T - N)\,avg_c + N.upperAvg}{T} = 80.6476$$

The final price lower bound,

$$p_{\text{lower}} = \frac{(T - N)\,avg_c + N.lowerAvg}{T} = 74.7976$$

Upper bound on number of target shares

$$= n^B \frac{p_{\text{upper}}}{p_{tgt}}$$

$$= 100000 \times \frac{80.6476}{60.0}$$

$$= 134413 \text{ shares (with 95\% confidence)}$$

Lower bound on number of target shares

$$= n^B \frac{p_{\text{lower}}}{p_{tgt}}$$

$$= 100000 \times \frac{74.7976}{60.0}$$

$$= 129,917 \text{ shares (with 95\% confidence)}$$

Note that in the preceding example, a volatility assumption is made for the bidder stock. Therefore, a realistic value for the volatility leads to good estimates. A reasonable approach to determining the volatility to use is to look at the implied volatility of the options on the bidder stock and choose the volatility corresponding to the contract with the most appropriate strike and expiration.

SHORT SELLING

As discussed in the introduction, the uptick rule makes it harder to short the stock. Until some time ago, a trading technique called *married puts* allowed the traders to sidestep the rules that prevented short sales when a stock's price was falling steadily. The strategy involved the following steps. First, buy a deep-in-the-money put with the closest maturity date. Then, tender for the shares. Now we are theoretically long the stock and can therefore sell it without waiting for the uptick. This loophole has, however, been detected and is now disallowed by the SEC.

In another approach to circumvent the uptick rule, one may also enter into a stock swap, receiving the acquirer's stock in exchange for cash. Now we are long the stock and can therefore sell the stock without the uptick rule restriction. To settle, we buy the acquirer's stock in the market and return it or pay the stock returns. In turn, we would receive LIBOR with a haircut. Notice that this is similar to short selling except that we pay a premium for the stock.

SUMMARY

- The arbitrageur normally executes the paired transaction through a broker.
- Verifying the executions by pairing them is an approach fraught with inconsistencies. It makes sense for the arbitrageur to insist on a firm average spread or better.
- It is possible to put on a spread position during the pricing period and be perfectly hedged. In such situations, however, the exact position size of the target stock is gradually revealed.
- Putting on a spread position typically involves a short sale and must be executed in accordance with the uptick rule.

FURTHER READING MATERIAL

On Linear Programming and Network Flows

Chavatal, Vasek. *Linear Programming.* (New York: Freeman, 1983).

APPENDIX

DINIC'S ALGORITHM FOR MAXIMUM FLOW IN A NETWORK

In this section, we describe Dininc's algorithm for maximum flow on a network. The following are some additional concepts used in the description of the algorithm.

Blocking Flow

A flow on a network is a blocking flow if every path from source to sink contains a saturated edge (edge with full capacity flow through it). An example of a blocking flow is shown in Figure 10.4. Also note that the flow is not maximum. The optimal flow is shown in Figure 10.4.

Residual Graph

Associated with every feasible flow through the network is a weighted digraph called the *residual graph*. This is constructed in the following manner. Let C be the capacity of the edge connecting vertices A and B. Let F be the flow from A to B. The residual graph has a directed edge from A to B with capacity $C - F$ and another from B to A with capacity F. All edges with zero capacity are removed from the graph thus constructed. The resultant graph is the residual graph. An example of the residual graph corresponding to the problem and the blocking flow is shown in Figure 10.4.

Flow Augmenting Paths

A flow augmenting path is a path on the residual graph from source to sink. The maximum flow that can be sent through this path is limited by capacity of the edges in the path. It is equal to the smallest capacity of an edge along the path.

Dinic's Algorithm

The steps in Dinic's Algorithm are as follows:

1. Find a blocking flow for a given network.
2. Construct the residual graph corresponding to the current flow.
3. Find the shortest length augmenting path on the residual graph. (The length of the path is equal to the number of edges in it.) If such a path does not exist, then the current flow is the maximum flow.
4. If such a path exists, then augment the flow along the path. (Make the corrections to the flow graph and the residual graph.) Go to Step 3.

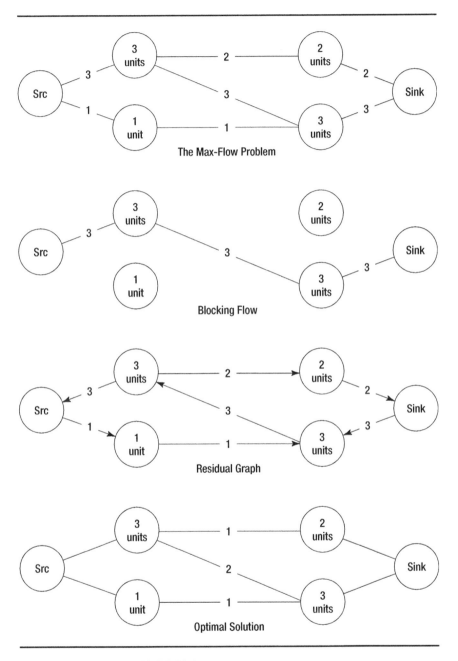

FIGURE 10.4 Max-Flow Algorithm.

LAZY ALLOCATION ALGORITHM

Dinic's algorithm is required for a general network. We hasten to add that the matching problem we are required to solve has some additional properties. To recognize that, we organize the trades on the stock being sold in ascending order (group A) and the trades on the stock being bought in descending order (Group B). Thus, each trade has a rank associated with it. Also, if there is a feasible edge between the ith vertex in group A and the jth vertex in group B, then there is a feasible edge between the ith vertex and all the vertices in group B with rank greater than j. Similarly, there is a feasible edge between the jth vertex in group B and all the vertices in group A with rank less than i. This is illustrated in the ordering of the nodes in Figure 10.2.

To perform lazy allocation, we start from the vertex with the lowest rank in group A and saturate the edge connecting it to the lowest possible rank in group B. When the entire trade quantity from the vertex is accounted for, we move on to the next vertex and do the same and work our way to the last vertex. The consequence of the lazy allocation is that on a graph with this structure, there is no flow augmenting path on the associated residual graph, and the allocation is optimal. An example of such an allocation method is demonstrated in Figure 10.2, configuration B.

Although there may not be any flow augmenting paths, there may be an alternate flow routing on the residual graph, such that the flow along the directed edge is zero. This implies that there could potentially be redundant optimal routings.

CHAPTER 11

The Market Implied Merger Probability

INTRODUCTION

The spread value in a merger deal is a measure of the profit potential of a trade. Knowledgeable players in the marketplace are likely to carefully assess the profit potential and inherent risks and put on a position according to their judgements. If the value of the spread is large and the risks inherent in the successful completion of the merger are small, then we can expect that the players would put on a large position causing the spread to narrow. If, however, the value of the spread narrows disproportionate to the risks, then we can expect some profit taking causing the spread to widen. If there are sufficient players in the marketplace engaging in risk arbitrage, the spread would then in some sense represent the consensus estimate of the risk involved in the deal and thereby the odds of successful completion of the merger. Therefore, it makes sense to construct models to estimate the odds of merger success taking the value of the spread into account.

In this chapter, we discuss a method to assess the probabilities of merger as reflected by the spread between the stock prices of the merging companies. The method is based firmly on the classical results of the Arrow-Debreu theory of contingent claims. The probabilities derived are called risk neutral probabilities.

Risk neutral probabilities calculated for a merger are in many ways similar to the implied volatility parameter encountered in option pricing. For purposes of option pricing, stock price movement is modeled as a lognormal process. One of the important parameters of the log-normal process is its standard deviation. This standard deviation is commonly termed *volatility*. The volatility of the underlying stock plays a crucial role in the pricing of an option. Conversely, the price of an option quoted in the marketplace implies a certain volatility that when plugged into the option pricing model results in the quoted option price. This volatility implied by the option price is called the *implied volatility*.

In an analogous fashion, the probability of merger success as implied by the observed spread may be calculated. Note that both implied volatility and the merger probability specify probability distributions. Furthermore, they are both calculated from values observed in the marketplace, and therein lies the similarity between the two constructs. A key question, however, pertains to the premise of the chapter. What is the value in knowing the market implied probability of merger? Well, if one has a view based on independent research that the true chance of merger success is better than the implied probability, then entering into a trade may have a good risk–reward profile. Thus, knowing the probability of merger can provide value in making investment decisions.

The implied probability of deal success can also prove useful in the area of risk management. The risk manager is typically charged with assessing the risk in multiple portfolios running multiple strategies. Unlike the risk arbitrage traders, risk managers are not disposed to know the intimate details of every deal in the risk arbitrage portfolio. Using the market-implied probabilities, the risk manager will be able to design meaningful value at risk (VAR) measures for such deals. The VAR plays a key role in determining the reserve capital requirements for a bank. The requirements for reserve capital are designed to help markets survive extreme conditions by making sure (to some extent) that the counterparties in a trade have enough reserve capital to meet their obligations. Ideally, we would like the reserve capital to be the proverbial Goldilocks value, not too little and not too much. If the risk measurement is too conservative, then we will need to post more reserves, leading to underutilization of capital. If it is too aggressive, then we may not have enough reserves to meet obligations during extreme moves. We will propose a practical value at risk measurement approach for risk arbitrage deals, based on the merger probabilities.

The chapter is organized as follows. First, we discuss briefly the Arrow-Debreu theory, which forms the basis for our probability measure. We then describe the single-step model for measuring merger probability success. The single-step model is then extended to multiple steps. Subsequently, we reconcile between the proposed theory and practice. This is followed by an example application to risk management.

IMPLIED PROBABILITIES AND ARROW-DEBREU THEORY

The purpose of this section is not so much to provide a formal description of the Arrow-Debreu theory as much as to provide a flavor for it. Let us consider the scenario that involves placing bets on a set of outcomes. Examples of such events could be a boxing match or a horse race. In these cases, the set of outcomes is finite and well defined. We will use the horse race example for purposes of illustration. Important to the discussion is the notion of betting. If, for example, the bet is placed in favor of a horse and it wins the race, then the reward is the payoff from the bet. If it happens to lose, then here, too, the reward is the payoff from the bet, except that the payoff is probably zero dollars. Thus, a bet is completely defined when we specify the payoff for every possible outcome. To place a bet, one has to put up the stake money. This is specified by the bookie.

The Arrow-Debreu theory states that the full and complete specification of bets with the stake money and the payoff for each outcome automatically implies a probability for a particular outcome.[1] Additionally, the stake

---

[1] The reasoning stems from the maximization of a linear utility function resulting in a linear program with constraints. The weights happen to be the values of the dual variables in the solution of the linear program. This work by Arrow and Debreu was awarded the Nobel Prize in Economics.

money must be the probability weighted payoff (also called the expected payoff) across all outcomes. Also, if it so happens that a single set of probability weights is not able to account for the entire set of bets, then arbitrage opportunities exist.

According to the theory, the probabilities are derived such that any two bets with the same expected payoff have the same current value. It may be that one of the two bets yields the expected payoff almost certainly and the risk associated with it is minimal when compared to the other bet. This scheme, however, treats both bets on an equal footing; that is, we are neutral to risk. For this reason, the set of probabilities that are implied by the definition of the bets are called risk neutral probabilities.

Continuing with the horse race example, let us say that the odds given by the bookie for the horse race is as follows: 3 to 5 in favor of NiceAndEasy, 2 to 3 in favor of WindSlicer, and 1 to 2 in favor of ButterBiscuit. For instance, a successful bet of one dollar on ButterBiscuit returns the stake plus two dollars, which is a total of three dollars. The terms of the bets are presented in Table 11.1.

Note that the first scenario described in Table 11.1 is the risk-free scenario where a deposit of x dollars with the bookie results in a payoff of one dollar no matter which horse wins. According to Arrow-Debreu theory, the bet amount must be a weighted combination of the payoffs. If the probability weights for each of the three horses winning are denoted as p_{ne}, p_{ws}, p_{bb}, then the following equations as given in matrix form must hold.

$$\begin{bmatrix} 1 & 1 & 1 \\ 8 & 0 & 0 \\ 0 & 5 & 0 \\ 0 & 0 & 3 \end{bmatrix} \cdot \begin{bmatrix} p_{ne} \\ p_{ws} \\ p_{bb} \end{bmatrix} = \begin{bmatrix} x \\ 3 \\ 2 \\ 1 \end{bmatrix}$$

TABLE 11.1 Terms of the Bet.

		Payoff from the Bets		
Bet scenario	Bet amount	NiceAndEasy wins	WindSlicer wins	ButterBiscuit wins
Risk-Free Scenario	x	1	1	1
Bet On NiceAndEasy	3	8	0	0
Bet on WindSlicer	2	0	5	0
Bet on ButterBiscuit	1	0	0	3

or specifically

$$p_{ne} + p_{ws} + p_{bb} = x$$
$$p_{ne} = 3/8 = 0.375$$
$$p_{ws} = 2/5 = 0.4$$
$$p_{bb} = 1/3 = 0.333$$

The value of x from the preceding equations is therefore $p_{ne} + p_{ws} + p_{bb}$ = 1.108. So, if we deposit close to a dollar and 11 cents with the bookie, we will get back a dollar. The loss for the bettor in this enterprise is therefore $100 \times (0.108/1.108)$, which is approximately 9.7 percent. In other words, on average the bookie gets to keep 10 cents on every dollar that is deposited as stakes. Normalizing the probability weights to add up to one, we now have

Probability of NiceAndEasy winning = 0.375/1.108 = .338
Probability of WindSlicer winning   = 0.4/1.108 = .361
Probability of ButterBiscuit winning = 0.333/1.108 = .301

Thus, WindSlicer is favored to win the race, with ButterBiscuit being the underdog.

Note that we started our example with the specification of the bets and their odds and have now derived the probabilities from it. Are the probabilities the true probabilities for the outcome of the race? Maybe, then again maybe not. This is, however, where the bookie will allow the bet to be made. In the case of the markets, unlike the example here, the price/stake amount of a bet is decided by the auctioning process. The price, therefore, represents the consensus opinion of the participants. In such situations it may be argued that the risk neutral probabilities represent the consensus of the market.

THE SINGLE-STEP MODEL

We are now ready to formulate the single-step model to calculate the probabilities implied by the spread. It is, however, good to remind ourselves of the implicit assumptions we make during the modeling process. First, putting on a spread involves a short position and we need to borrow stock. At times it may turn out that a particular stock is unavailable for borrow. However, for purposes of our model, we will assume that the stock is always available to borrow. Additionally, we also assume that there are no liquidity issues and that it is possible to put on a spread position in size at the current spread level observed in the market. This would imply that the transaction costs if any are negligible and may be assumed to be zero.

To construct our model, let us now go through the mechanics of a risk arbitrage trade. Initially, a spread position is created. We do this by establishing a short position in the target and a long position in the bidder, yielding a dollar value equal to the spread. The proceeds from the trades are reinvested at the risk-free rate. Let us call this spread at time zero S_0. Upon successful completion of the deal, the spread would converge to zero. The position is reversed for no additional cost at time T, and the reward earned by the investor will be $e^{rT} S_0$, with r being the interest rate. In case there is some cash paid out for the target shares, the payoff will be $e^{rT} S_0 + cash$. However, if the deal ends in a failure, the spread will not converge to zero as expected. Instead, it inflates to a value of, say, S_T. The position will still need to be reversed, and a cost equal to the spread at time T, S_T, is incurred. The net payoff in the event of deal failure is therefore $e^{rT} S_0 - S_T$. The discussion of the scenarios here is illustrated in a state diagram as shown in Figure 11.1.

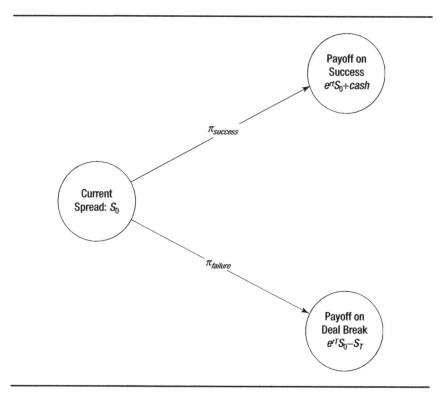

FIGURE 11.1   Single-Step Model.

The state diagram in Figure 11.1 comes with a few caveats. Very often, the fact that the deal is going to be unsuccessful is known much before the time it would take for successful completion, in which case, treating both the payoffs as if they are known at the same time would not be appropriate. For our purposes, however, we choose to reflect this difference in timing in the value of S_T while keeping T a constant. Later on in the multistep model formulation, we will eliminate the need to estimate S_T. Therefore, keeping T the same for both the success and failure scenarios does not affect the outcome of the model.

Recall that the initial cost of setting up the trade was zero. By the no arbitrage condition the expected payoff is also zero. Writing out the equations, we have

$$\pi_{\text{success}}(e^{rT}S_0 + \text{cash}) + \pi_{\text{failure}}(e^{rT}S_0 - S_T) = 0 \qquad (11.1)$$

$$\pi_{\text{success}} + \pi_{\text{failure}} = 1 \qquad (11.2)$$

where π_{success} and π_{failure} are the risk-neutral probabilities of successful merger and failed merger, respectively. Solving the two equations, we have

$$\pi_{\text{failure}} = e^{rT}(S_0 + e^{-rT}\text{cash}) / (S_T + \text{cash}) \qquad (11.3)$$

Note here that in the derivation of the one-step model we apply the Arrow-Debreu ideas to the spread. For the curious mind, the same results may be obtained by applying the Arrow-Debreu ideas to the individual stocks in question, also. The derivation of the formulas for the model using the individual stocks is presented in the appendix.

In Equation 11.3 for failure probability, all the values are known or observable except for S_T, the spread in the future if the deal happens to break. The value for this spread is anybody's guess. Unless a reasonable value for the deal break spread is known, the one-step model as it stands is of not much use. We deal with this issue in the multistep model.

THE MULTISTEP MODEL

The multistep model relates the changes in the risk-neutral probability to the dynamics of the spread movement. In this case, it is crucial to have an estimate of deal break probability on the eve of the announcement. If we are able to assess the probability of successful merger on the eve of the announcement, the value may be updated periodically based on the spread dynamics. This eliminates the need to guess at the deal break spread and thus mitigates the problem of the one-step model. We now proceed to describe the model.

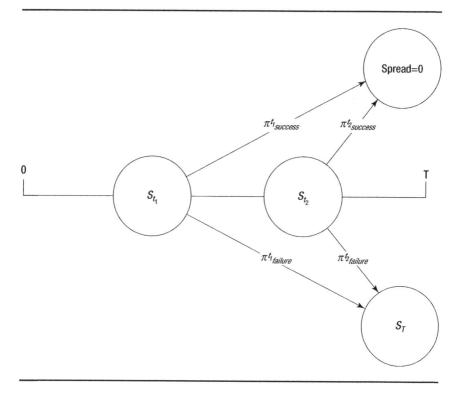

FIGURE 11.2   Multistep Model.

Let t_1 and t_2 be points in the interval $[0,T]$ and $t_2 > t_1$. We denote the probabilities of failed merger at times t_1 and t_2 by, $\pi^{t_1}_{failure}, \pi^{t_2}_{failure}$ and the spreads by S_{t_1}, S_{t_2}, respectively. See Figure 11.2.
Applying the one-step model, we have

$$\pi^{t_1}_{failure} = e^{r(T-t_1)}(S_{t_1} + e^{-r(T-t_1)}\text{cash}) \,/\, (S_T + \text{cash}) \qquad (11.4)$$

$$\pi^{t_2}_{failure} = e^{r(T-t_2)}(S_{t_2} + e^{-r(T-t_2)}\text{cash}) \,/\, (S_T + \text{cash}) \qquad (11.5)$$

Dividing one by the other, we have

$$\pi^{t_1}_{failure} \,/\, \pi^{t_2}_{failure} = e^{r(t_2-t_1)}(S_{t_1} + e^{-r(T-t_1)}\text{cash}) \,/\, (S_{t_2} + e^{-r(T-t_2)}\text{cash}) \quad (11.6)$$

To get a better feel for what the equation signifies, let us consider the situation of a pure stock-for-stock deal without a cash component. Making the cash to zero, the equation in this case reduces to

$$\pi_{\text{failure}}^{t_2} \Big/ \pi_{\text{failure}}^{t_1} = e^{r(t_1-t_1)} S_{t_1} \Big/ S_{t_1} \qquad (11.7)$$

Taking logarithms on both sides, we now have

$$\log\left(\pi_{\text{failure}}^{t_2}\right) - \log\left(\pi_{\text{failure}}^{t_1}\right) = -r(t_2 - t_1) + \log\left(S_{t_2}\right) - \log\left(S_{t_1}\right) \qquad (11.8)$$

Let us see how this equation may be interpreted. First, when $t_2 - t_1$ is a small quantity, the above becomes a difference equation. The left-hand side is the difference in the logarithms of the probabilities. The negative logarithm of probabilities can be interpreted as a measure of information content. Therefore, the left-hand side may be interpreted as the change in information content between the times t_1 and t_2. The right-hand side has a term consisting of the difference in the logarithm of the spreads. This is, in fact, the unrealized profit per target share. The other term on the right-hand side represents the risk-free return. Therefore, the equation may be interpreted as saying that any return in excess of the risk-free rate is equal to the change in the information content, that is, the reduction in the uncertainty of deal break.

Once we have the initial probability value, that is, π_{failure}^0, all the probabilities in the interval $[0,T]$ can be evaluated using the difference Equation 11.8. We have thus eliminated the requirement to make a guess at the spread value in case of deal break. This is replaced with the assessment of the initial deal break probability. As a practical matter, the risk-free rate values in Equations 11.7 and 11.8 are rather negligible. We can therefore set $r = 0$ in our calculations.

LOGARITHMS AND INFORMATION THEORY

The interpretation of the negative logarithm of probabilities as the information content was originally proposed by Claude E. Shannon in his groundbreaking article "A Mathematical Theory of Communication," published in 1948.[2] Shannon was then working at Bell Laboratories. The powerful ideas describing the ways to measure rates of information flow very soon became a discipline in its own right called information theory. As a matter of fact, the word *bit* (as in bits per second) that is so commonly used today is attributed to Shannon.

[2]"A Mathematical Theory of Communication," *Bell System Technical Journal* 27 (July and October 1948): 379–423; 623–656.

The initial deal break probability can be naively estimated using a number of robust statistical methods based on past data relating to deal announcements and successful completions. Alternately, an assessment of the fundamentals of the two merging companies can be used to arrive at the deal break probability. Yet another approach could be to base it simply on the instantaneous reduction of the spread on deal announcement. The average of the logarithm of the spread for the 10 days just prior to deal announcement could be used as the logarithm of the spread corresponding to a failure probability of 1.

RECONCILING THEORY AND PRACTICE

To see how the theory bears out in practice, let us look at some implications of the preceding model. According to the theory, the expectation is that the spread will converge to zero in the case of successful completion of merger. Alternately, we expect it blow up or widen in case the merger does not go through. We present both examples and counterexamples. In cases where the model might not hold, we also provide possible reasons as to why that would be the case. All the examples presented are taken from the merger boom period of the late 1990s.

Also, the key value in the theory relates to the logarithm of the spread. If the logarithm of the spread goes down in a linear fashion, then the spread goes down in an exponential fashion. As a matter of fact, in the case of mergers with no glitches along the way, it is not unreasonable to expect the logarithm of the spread to decrease in a linear fashion. We could therefore expect the spread to exponentially approach zero as the merger date nears.

Now when the spread goes to zero, the logarithm of the spread goes to negative infinity. In practice, we may assume a lower bound to the value of the spread between the two stocks to be at least equal to or greater than the bid-ask spread between them. At best, the spread could go to a penny. The logarithm of the spread for a penny is –4.6. That would be about the lowest value that we could expect for the logarithm of the spread.

With that said, let us look at some real-life deals. We start by looking at some mergers where the spread behavior follows the model. Figure 11.3 shows examples where the theory holds. Figure 11.3a is a plot of the spread for a successful merger. The bidder in this case was Newell Company, and the target was Rubbermaid Corporation. The ratio for exchange was 0.7883. The deal was announced on October 21, 1998, and completed March 24, 1999. Notice from the figure that it is conceivable that we could fit an exponential to the overall profile of the spread.

Figure 11.3b is a plot of the spread of an unsuccessful merger. The bidder was American Home Products (AHP), and the target was Monsanto

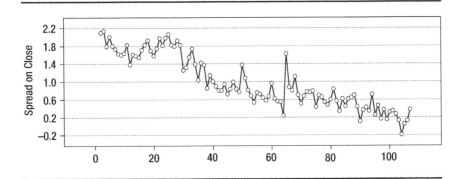

FIGURE 11.3A   Successful Merger (NWL-RBD).

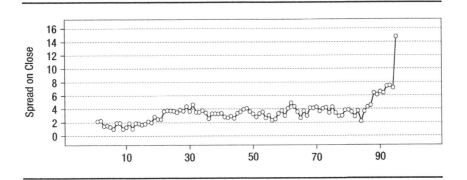

FIGURE 11.3B   Unsuccessful Merger (AHP-MTC).

Corp. (MTC). The exchange ratio was 1.15. The deal was announced June 1, 1998. It became obvious that the deal was a failed deal around October 13, 1998. The plot of the spread in the graph is for these dates. Notice that the spread does not converge at all. This is indicative of the risk involved in this particular merger. When it becomes obvious that the deal will not go through, the spread in fact blows up.

We also present cases where the theory does not bear out. Figure 11.4a is a plot of an inverted spread. The bidder in this case was Venetor Group (Z). The target was Sports Authority (TSA). The exchange ratio was 0.8. The deal was announced May 7, 1998, and it became apparent that the deal was unsuccessful around September 10, 1998. Note that the spread in this case takes on negative values. The logarithm of the spread in this case is undefined. It is not possible to apply the theory here. Such a situation is

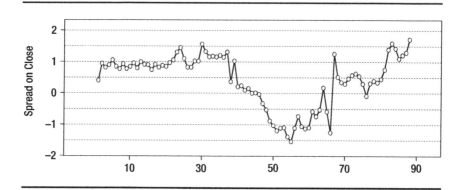

FIGURE 11.4A   Inverted Spread (Z-TSA).

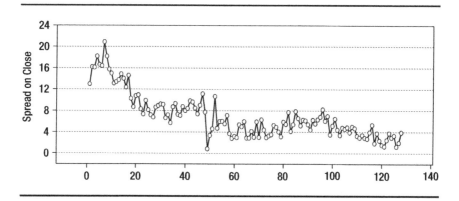

FIGURE 11.4B   Unconverged Spread (BRK-GRN).

possible if there are not enough arbitrageurs participating in the merger. As a consequence, the spread dynamics do not imply anything.

Figure 11.4b is a plot of an unconverged spread. The bidder in this case was Berkshire Hathaway (whose chairman was the famous Warren Buffet). The target was General Re, a reinsurance company. The deal was announced June 19, 1998, and completed December 21, 1998. It is interesting to note that the spread on close was about $ 4.00; that is, the convergence to zero did not happen. To see why that would be the case, note the fact that Berkshire stocks were priced very high, and the exchange ratio was about 0.0035; that is, for every thousand shares of General Re we would need 3.5 shares of Berkshire to be perfectly hedged. This awkward exchange ratio is hard to achieve given the average per-trade volume of General Re and Berkshire. Thus, the liquidity of the stocks involved increases the execution risk and caused the inefficiency.

We now apply the theory to the INTC–LEVL example discussed in Chapter 10. Figures 11.5a and b are plots of the spread and the probability implied by the spread as of the close. The initial probability is determined as the percentage by which the spread narrows on deal announcement with respect to the spread calculated on the 10-day average prices of the securities. In this case it turns out to be close to 30 percent; that is, the spread narrowed by about 70 percent on deal announcement. Note that the probabilities calculated follow the spread values very closely. This results in a very noisy picture. It is conceivable that the probabilities do not vary as much. It is therefore useful to use some smoothing function on the spread before evaluating the implied probabilities. We will discuss this in greater detail in Chapter 12.

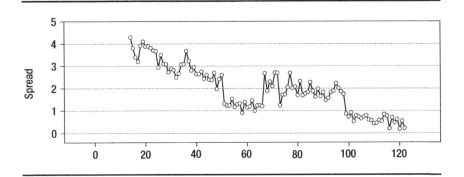

FIGURE 11.5A   Spread (INTC-LEVL).

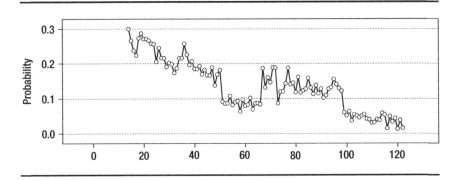

FIGURE 11.5B   Probability of Deal Break (INTC-LEVL).

RISK MANAGEMENT

One of the important tasks in risk measurement is the estimation of VAR, an acronym for *value at risk*.

VAR Measurement

Let us now detail what we mean by VAR measurement starting with the outcome of the measurement process. The outcome is a statement as follows: "Under usual market conditions, there is a 2.5-percent chance of losing X dollars in one day given the current list of positions." The value X is the value at risk and is based on the current (day's close) mark to market. The value of X is typically based on the statistics of the daily market movement in the past two to three years—that is, the distribution of price movements—and, more importantly, on the correlation between the price movements of various assets. The exercise is therefore to determine what the likely value of X is.

Also note that there is nothing magical about use of the 2.5-percent value in the VAR statement. It is an artifact left from the cultural conditioning of dealing with Gaussian distributions and represents two standard deviations in the Gaussian case. That value could therefore be 1 percent or any number that one fancies.

Another key aspect of the preceding statement is the use of the phrase, "usual market conditions." This is because the measurement approach that works under usual market conditions is not sound under extreme market conditions. This is because the correlations that may be considered as relatively stable under usual market conditions become erratic under extreme market conditions causing the VAR approach to break down.

Applying the same reasoning based on the correlation between asset prices, it is easy to deduce that commonly applicable methods to measure the VAR on a portfolio may not be used in the case of risk arbitrage. The announcement of the deal causes a qualitative shift in the way the two companies are viewed in the marketplace. The historical correlation between them is no longer relevant. The market dynamic now also reflects the possibility of merger between the two companies and there is an increased level of correlation between the returns of the bidder and target stocks. Therefore, any VAR methodology that relies on long-term historical correlation is rendered inappropriate.

Furthermore, use of the historical correlation could potentially inflate the VAR numbers, increasing risk capital requirements, resulting in an unrealistic increased cost of doing business. This leads us to look for reasonable ways to evaluate the value at risk involved in risk arbitrage trades.

The risk arbitrage trade at hand can be viewed in two ways. On event of deal failure, it is equivalent to holding two separate securities, and traditional VAR methodologies will apply. However, when the deal is on, the risk is mostly due to the spread volatility, and the value at risk is best obtained by measuring the spread volatility. Thus, based on the view we choose to adopt, we now have two VAR values. We now reconcile between the two views and arrive at a final VAR number by weighing each scenario. Fortunately for us, the consensus probabilities of deal success and failure provide us with a ready mechanism by which to weigh the two views.

Putting things more precisely, each of the two views may be associated with a return distribution describing the probability of return of the trade in the next time period. The overall probability distribution is then a weighted sum of the two distributions, the weights corresponding to the probability of deal success and deal failure, respectively. Distributions that are constructed as a weighted sum of other distributions are called *mixed density distributions*.

To better understand the model, let us consider the process of drawing a sample from a mixture distribution. This is actually a two-step process. In the first step, we randomly choose the distribution from the available set of distributions. The choice is guided by the probability weights assigned to each distribution in the set. In the next step, we draw a random sample from the chosen distribution.

Applying the mixture model to our situation, the probability of an outcome x dollars or lower is given by the distribution function shown in Equation 11.9

$$F(x) = \pi_{\text{success}} \Phi_{\text{spread}}(x) + \pi_{\text{failure}} \Phi_{\text{stockPortfolio}}(x) \qquad (11.9)$$

where Φ_{spread} is the distribution of spread returns, and $\Phi_{\text{stockPortfolio}}$ is the distribution of the returns assuming that there is no deal. The failure and success probabilities serve as weights. Thus, given a value of x dollars, we can find the probability that the returns will be less than or equal to x using the above formula.

Note that VAR value is that value of x that results in the probability value of 2.5 percent in Equation 11.9. Additionally, the distribution function like every other distribution function is a nondecreasing function. As a consequence, the VAR value may be deduced by applying a standard binary search method. Thus, knowledge of the consensus probability estimates of deal success and failure may be used to calculate the VAR in risk arbitrage trades.

Event Risk Management

Oftentimes in risk arbitrage, the outcome of merger success or deal break may hinge on a single event like the shareholders' vote or a court decision.

The arbitrageur may find the reward adequate but the risk too high. In such situations, the arbitrageur can protect himself against a widening spread through the use of options.

Typically, the target stock experiences higher volatility relative to the bidder stock. The common strategy under these circumstances is to purchase a put on the target stock, thus protecting against a steep drop in the price of the target. While the price paid to enter into the hedge eats away at some of the profit in the trades, the risk due to the put purchase is a lot lower.

It may also be that the deal poses a high degree of risk for some time. Once the event resolves itself favorably, the risk of deal break diminishes substantially. The timing, strike, and expiration of the put used will therefore depend on the appetite for risk and the degree of risk aversion of the arbitrageur.

It must therefore be noted that while at the surface the risk arbitrage process seems cut and dried, there is still a substantial amount of decision making and judgment calls that are left to the discretion of the arbitrageur.

SUMMARY

- The risk neutral probability of merger is the probability implied by the observed spread between the bidder and target firms.
- It is similar to the implied volatility parameter for options.
- The evolution of the risk neutral probability of merger can be related to the spread dynamics.
- It is useful in the design of more appropriate value at risk measures.

FURTHER READING MATERIAL

Risk-Neutral Probability

Jarrow, R. and S. Turnbull *Derivative Securities*, (Cincinnati, Ohio: 2nd Edition. South Western Publishing, 2000).

APPENDIX

Notation

p_0^A	Price of security A on the eve of merger announcement
p_0^B	Price of security B on the eve of merger announcement
p_T^{AB}	Price of combined entity at time T
p_T^A	Price of security A in case of deal break at time T
p_T^B	Price of security B in case of deal break at time T
$\pi_{success}$	Probability of successful merger
$\pi_{failure}$	Probability of deal break
γ	Ratio

We now construct Table 11.2 similar to Table 11.1.

TABLE 11.2

Investment Scenario	Initial Price	Payoff (Price at Time T)	
		Merger Successful	*Merger Failed*
Risk-Free	e^{-rT}	1	1
Buy Stock A	p_0^A	p_T^{AB}	p_T^A
Buy Stock B	γp_0^B	$p_T^{AB} + \text{cash}$	γp_T^B

The Arrow-Debreu equations that need to be satisfied written in matrix form is as follows:

$$\begin{bmatrix} 1 & 1 \\ p_T^{AB} & p_T^A \\ p_T^{AB} + \text{cash} & \gamma p_T^B \end{bmatrix} \begin{bmatrix} \pi'_{success} \\ \pi'_{failure} \end{bmatrix} = \begin{bmatrix} e^{-rT} \\ p_0^A \\ p_0^B \end{bmatrix}$$

Solving for the values of $\pi'_{success}$ and $\pi'_{failure}$ and normalizing so that they add up to 1, we have

$$\pi_{failure} = [e^{rT}(p_0^A - \gamma p_0^B) + \text{cash}] / [(p_T^A - \gamma p_T^B) + \text{cash}]$$

Applying the fact that

$$S_0 = p_0^A - \gamma p_0^B$$
$$S_T = p_T^A - \gamma p_T^B$$

We have

$$\pi_{\text{failure}} = (e^{rT} S_0 + \text{cash}) / (S_T + \text{cash}).$$

CHAPTER 12

Spread Inversion

INTRODUCTION

In Chapter 11 we discussed that the risk neutral probabilities of merger can be evaluated from the value of the spread as observed in the marketplace. The reasoning was that market forces that affect the value of the spread take into account the risk of deal completion. It is probably true that in most cases the deal completion risk is the predominant factor affecting the spread dynamics. However, the spread is also subject to idiosyncratic movement on the part of any one of the two stocks in question. This movement can be due to a variety of reasons that have nothing to do with the deal completion risk and hence contributes to what we shall term *noise* in the evaluation of the spread-implied probabilities. This fact is rather evident from the raw plot of the spreads.

Some of the reasons for this behavior could be due to the bid-ask spread of the individual stocks and the order of the buys and sells as they occur on each individual stock. It could also be due to the market maker, looking to adjust inventory. The market maker may move the price sufficiently higher or lower albeit on a temporary basis to produce the desired supply or demand in the stock and thereby adjust his inventory levels. Another reason for the spread movement could be attributed to short covering on the target stock especially right after the merger announcement. Therefore, when attempting to evaluate the deal break probabilities, we need to bear in mind that the observed spread is not a consequence of the deal risk alone.

However, if the deal risk is the predominant driver of the spread dynamics, the other effects may be treated as noise and filtered using classical filtering methods. In this chapter, we propose the Kalman filter for the task. The primary reason for proposing the Kalman filter is that it is robust and easy to use. Unlike Weiner filtering methods, which are valid only for stationary stochastic signals, the Kalman filter may be applied to a wide variety of situations without restriction. This property conveniently precludes us from coming to any conclusions on the stationarity of the spread and makes it a suitable candidate method.

A comprehensive introduction to the Kalman filter is provided in Chapter 4. However, for sake of continuity we will summarize the method here in a few sentences. The idea of Kalman filtering revolves around the notion of state of the system. The process involves a sequence of state predictions followed by observations. The predictions are then reconciled with the observations to obtain the best estimate of the state. Applying the idea to our situation, let the state correspond to the logarithm of the spread. This process then translates as follows. First, we make a prediction of the next value for the log-spread and follow this with an observation after the elapsed time. The predicted log-spread and the observed log-spread are then reconciled to form the best estimate of the spread at that time instance. The process is then repeated for the next time step.

Based on the discussion here, it is now obvious that Kalman filter design for our problem involves two main steps. First, we need to design the prediction method that we plan to use, to provide us with an a priori estimate of the state. Next, we need to model the observation process. The outcome from the observation modeling process is a means of observing the state along with a method to estimate the error variance in the observation. Once we have the prediction and observation, the Kalman filtering process provides us with the means to reconcile between them to come up with an estimate of the state; that is, the logarithm of the spread. This value can in turn be used to estimate the spread implied probability of deal break. Let us now discuss the modeling process for the prediction and observation equations.

THE PREDICTION EQUATION

The prediction equation is essentially an equation specifying the state transition for the Kalman filter. Since in our case the state corresponds to the logarithm of the spread, the state equation in our case involves coming up with a prediction scheme for the value of the spread at the next time step. We of course have at our disposal all the past values of the spread right up to the current time step. Let us therefore discuss how we can achieve that.

In order to motivate our choice for the state equation, we recall the difference equation from the previous chapter.

$$\log\left(\pi_{\text{failure}}^{t_2}\right) - \log\left(\pi_{\text{failure}}^{t_1}\right) = -r\left(t_2 - t_1\right) + \log\left(S_{t_2}\right) - \log\left(S_{t_1}\right) \quad (12.1)$$

The left-hand side of the equation is equivalent to the rate of information flow. The right-hand side is the return in excess of the risk-free rate. The implication is that under static interest rate conditions and a constant rate of information arrival at the market, the rate of decay of the spread would be a constant. However, the various milestones leading to the merger like the filing of documents, the proxy vote, and so forth, all happen at discrete times. So, how realistic is the assumption of a constant rate of information flow? It turns out that it is not terribly unrealistic. When the merger announcement is made and events are set into motion, it creates an expectation in the marketplace as to the timing of the various milestones leading to the merger. If a day passes without any news contrary to expectation, then it strengthens the expectations. In that sense, the mere passage of time may be construed as providing information leading to the strengthening of expectations—one of the very rare cases in the market where no news is considered good news.

A constant rate of information flow, according to the model, carries with it the implication that the logarithm of the spread approaches zero in a linear fashion. In fact, this would be a very reasonable assumption, if the deal were to proceed without any hiccups. However, given the vicissitudes of the deal process, such an assumption might prove to be untenable. Nevertheless, it may still be reasonable to assume that the logarithm of the spread is piecewise linear; that is, the rate of spread reduction is about the same as observed in the recent past. Therefore, we model the spread at the next time instant to be the current spread decremented by the instantaneous rate of reduction of the spread. The state equation is given as

$$X_t = X_{t-1} + \Delta_{t-1} + \varepsilon_t \qquad (12.2)$$

where Δ_{t-1} is the instantaneous rate of change of the spread. Note that Equation 12.2 can also be viewed as the first two terms of a Taylor expansion of the spread about X_{t-1}.

This, therefore, brings us to the requirement of specifying a scheme to evaluate the instantaneous rate of change of the spread, Δ_{t-1}. A naive method would be to use the correction rate of the past time step given by

$$\Delta_{t-1} = \hat{X}_{t-1|t-1} - \hat{X}_{t-2|t-2} \qquad (12.3)$$

A little more sophisticated method would be to take the minimum variance weighted average of the past two correction rates given by

$$\Delta_{t-1} = r_t\left(\hat{X}_{t-1|t-1} - \hat{X}_{t-2|t-2}\right) + \left(1 - r_t\right)\left(\hat{X}_{t-2|t-2} - \hat{X}_{t-3|t-3}\right) \qquad (12.4)$$

where r_t is the weight. Alternately, one could obtain an estimate of the correction rate by taking the mean correction rate over the past d time steps; that is,

$$\Delta_{t-1} = \frac{\left(\hat{X}_{t-1|t-1} - \hat{X}_{t-2|t-2}\right) +, \dots, + \left(\hat{X}_{t-d|t-d} - \hat{X}_{t-1-d|t-1-d}\right)}{d} \qquad (12.5)$$

$$\Delta_{t-1} = \frac{\left(\hat{X}_{t-1|t-1} - \hat{X}_{t-1-d|t-1-d}\right)}{d}$$

Thus, the process of evaluating the instantaneous rate of reduction of the spread could vary depending on d, the number of time steps in the past that we use in our estimation. Consequently, we could have different state equations corresponding to different values of d, the lag parameter, and for each such state equation, a version of the Kalman filter could be implemented.

But which one of the state equations is most suited for our purpose? Let us defer this question for now and address it a little later in the chapter.

Another point that is noteworthy in the modeling of the prediction equation is the fact that the actual equation used is different for each time step. The exact values for the coefficients in the prediction equation are estimated at each time step based on the instantaneous rate of spread reduction. This is a little different from typical Kalman filter implementations that have a fixed prediction equation with fixed coefficients. We are now ready to move on to the observation equation.

THE OBSERVATION EQUATION

The observation at a given time instant is the logarithm of the spread. Associated with an observation is a measure of the error. The magnitude of this error is quantified in terms of the error variance. The observation equation is written as

$$Y_t = X_t + \eta_t \qquad (12.6)$$

where Y_t is the logarithm of the observed spread at time t and η_t is the observation error with zero mean and variance $\sigma_{\eta_t}^2$. We now therefore need to estimate the variance of our observation.

To estimate the variance of the observation, we draw on the notion of realized volatility. Realized volatility is essentially an empirical volatility measure that sums the squared tick-by-tick returns over a given period. The construction of the realized volatility measure is based on some theoretical results of integrated volatility defined in the context of continuous stochastic processes. A detailed discussion on realized volatility measures and its scaling properties can be found in the reference material.

Bear in mind that if we use the realized volatility as a measure of the variance in the observation, then we would need access to tick data. The spread can then be evaluated on a tick-by-tick basis and the sum of squared returns on the spread could be used as a measure of observation variance. In the absence of tick data we use the following approximation to estimate the realized volatility measure. Initially, the four spreads corresponding to the open high low and close prices for the day of the two stocks are computed. Note that the times in which the two stocks registered their highs could be different; nevertheless, we treat them as if the highs were registered simultaneously. The sum of squared returns on the spread is calculated on the two possible spread paths; namely, open-high-low-close and open-low-high-close. The smaller of the two values is then chosen to be the variance of the observation. The question the reader might ask at this point is, "Is this really the variance of the error in the observation?" It is probably not. However, the variances thus calculated are not used to price any instrument. It should suffice that the measured variances are proportional to the actual error variances and that the relative order of the errors associated with the observations is preserved. This ensures that the weighting of the observations in the evaluation of the state estimate in done in a consistent manner resulting in state estimates that seem to be satisfactory.

To get an intuitive feel for the volatility measure, consider the following. As the spread gets closer to zero, the bid-ask spread of the individual stocks measured as a percentage of the spread between the two stocks becomes higher. It then gets increasingly harder to tell whether the change in spread is real or due to microstructure or bid-ask effects. Thus, as the spread reduces, we should expect an increase in its variance.

APPLYING THE KALMAN FILTER

Summarizing the discussions so far, in order to apply the Kalman filtering approach to smooth the spread, we went through the exercise of modeling the prediction equation and the observation equation. The Kalman state in our situation corresponds to the logarithm of the true spread, and the observation corresponds to the logarithm spread as observed in the market.

The state equation as applicable in our situation is given as

$$X_t = X_{t-1} + \Delta_{t-1} + \varepsilon_t \qquad (12.7)$$

where X_t is the state at time t, Δ_{t-1} is the time derivative of X_{t-1}, and ε_t is the state noise. The time derivative Δ_{t-1} may be estimated by measuring the average change in the spread over different lag values. The observation equation is given by

$$Y_t = X_t + \eta_t \qquad (12.8)$$

where Y_t is the observation and η_t is the observation noise with zero mean and variance of $\sigma_{\eta_t}^2$.

With this information we are now ready to apply the Kalman-filtering ideas in a recipe-like fashion (as discussed in Chapter 4). We list the recipe below once again for sake of continuity. The a priori estimate of the state at time t given all observations up to time $t - 1$ is denoted as $\hat{X}_{t|t-1}$, and the posteriori estimate of the state at time t given all the observations up to time t is given as $\hat{X}_{t|t}$. The various steps are then as follows:

1. Evaluate $\hat{X}_{t|t-1}$ and $\text{var}\left(\hat{X}_{t|t-1}\right)$ using the state equation.
2. Find the observation Y_t and $\text{var}\left(Y_t\right)$ by observing the system.
3. Evaluate K_t, also known as the Kalman gain, which will be used to obtain the linear minimum error variance estimate.
4. Evaluate $\hat{X}_{t|t}$ given by $\hat{X}_{t|t-1} + K_t\left(Y_t - \hat{X}_{t|t-1}\right)$
5. Finally, evaluate $\text{var}\left(\hat{X}_{t|t}\right)$

These steps are repeated for the next time step. The exact formulas to use for the various steps are derived in simplified form in the appendix.

MODEL SELECTION

Note that based on the preceding scheme, we have multiple models for the prediction equation. The differentiating factor amongst them is d, the lag factor used in the estimation of the instantaneous error correction rates. For each of the prediction equations, we can implement a unique Kalman filter-implementation. We therefore need to choose the implementation that is most appropriate; that is, we need to make an appropriate choice for the parameter d.

The principle guiding our choice for the lag value d is the maintenance of the delicate balance between prediction and observation. Relying overly on the prediction would mean that we rely excessively on our model and do not give enough weight to what is observed in practice. However, relying too much on the observation would mean that we do not have any view whatsoever on where the spread must be and so must rely excessively on the noisy observation. The right model choice achieves a happy medium between the two extremes. Let us therefore look at how we can quantify this notion of a happy medium.

The basic idea is to work with the two sources of error; namely, the measurement/observation error and the state transition prediction error. We denote the measurement cost as the sum of all measurement errors and the prediction cost as the sum of all the prediction errors. More precisely, if $X_1, X_2, X_3, \ldots, X_n$ are the estimated states of the Kalman filter,

$Y_1, Y_2, Y_3, \ldots, Y_n$, the measurements, and $Z_1, Z_2, Z_3, \ldots, Z_n$, the predicted values from the state equation, then

$$\text{measurement cost} = \sum_{i=1}^{n} \left(X_i - Y_i \right)^2$$

$$\text{prediction cost} = \sum_{i=1}^{n} \left(X_i - Z_i \right)^2$$

These cost functions may be considered the measures of effectiveness of the measurement and the state transition models. A high prediction cost indicates a poor prediction model. Similarly, a high observation cost indicates a poor observation model. If the two models must be equally effective, it makes sense to require that the values of the two cost functions be more or less the same.

Additionally, we also know that the Kalman estimate for the state is a convex combination of the measured and predicted states; that is, given k_i to be the Kalman gain at the ith time step, we have

$$X_i = (1 - k_i)Z_i + k_i X_i \tag{12.9}$$

The discussion on model selection in the case of smoothing functions can be viewed as a situation where we attempt to separate the signal from noise given a sum of both. On the one hand, we can be very conservative and treat every kink as meaningful and separate out very little as noise. On the other hand, we can throw the baby out with the bathwater and oversmooth the given signal, discarding part of the signal along with the noise. The model selection criterion above provides us with a methodology to achieve a balance between both extremes.

This dependency on the measured and predicted states requires both the measurement model and the prediction model to be fairly precise. Having one of them to be very precise and the other to be erroneous leads us to overly rely on one or the other and is likely to produce a mediocre result. Thus, in some sense there is a trade-off to be made between the observation and prediction costs, and the reduction of one of the costs at the expense of the other is highly undesirable.

With this motivation, we define the cost function associated with a Kalman filter to be

$$\text{cost function} = \text{measurement cost} + \text{prediction cost} \quad (12.10)$$

This cost function serves to keep the system honest. If in an attempt to reduce the cost function, we try to reduce the prediction cost, it would be all right as long as it does not increase the measurement cost and vice versa. The best choice for our prediction equation is therefore the one that results in the minimum value for this cost function.

To demonstrate the approach, let us apply it to a real-life situation. Figure 12.1 is a plot of the spread and the corresponding Kalman smoother for various lags. The bidder in this case is McKesson Inc., and the target is HBO

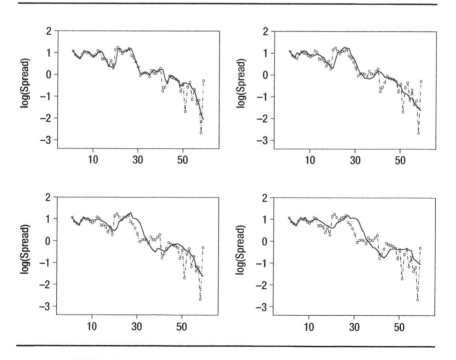

FIGURE 12.1 Kalman Filter Implementations (MCK-HBOC).

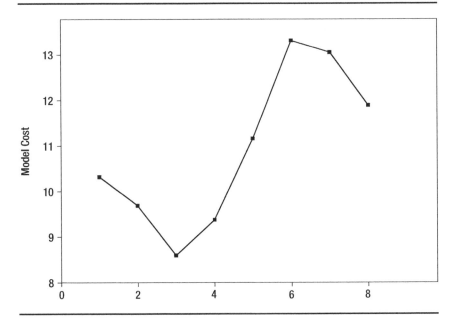

FIGURE 12.2   Model Choice (MCK-HBOC).

and Company. The exchange ratio is 0.37. The deal was announced October 19, 1998, and completed January 13, 1999. Notice that smaller lags tend to follow the data more closely. Increasing the lag results in greater smoothing and greater deviations from the data.

We also have a plot of the cost function as discussed for various lags. See Figure 12.2.

Note that the minimum cost value occurs at lag 3. A visual examination of the smoothed series for lag 3 against the series for other lags shows that it is indeed a reasonable choice.

Thus, a low value for the lag parameter d implies a noisy set of state estimates, making the Kalman filter very sensitive to the observations. Alternately, a high value for the lag parameter d denotes a smoother set of states and the observations are largely ignored. The most suitable value for the lag parameter is one that minimizes the cost function.

APPLICATIONS TO TRADING

Along with the smoothed version of the spread, at every time instant, the Kalman filter also estimates the error standard deviation at each point. This can be treated as error bands, about a mean estimate, similar to bollinger bands in technical analysis. Trading can be undertaken when the observed spread is on the upper and lower fringes of the band.

We, however, add a note of caution. When the spread widens to the upper fringe of the band, it may be because there is some deterioration in the fundamentals of the merger and may not be just an aberration. Therefore, one needs to exercise extreme caution when putting the spread on. The matter is straightforward when timing the unwind. If the observed spread is near the bottom fringe of the band, then one can safely unwind the position and get back into it again at a higher spread level.

Illustrated in Figure 12.3 is a plot of the spread, the Kalman smoother, and the error bands. The bidder in this case was Alza Pharmaceuticals. The target was Sequus Pharmaceuticals. The exchange ratio was 0.4 share. The deal was announced October 5, 1998, and completed March 17, 1999.

Last, it is important to bear in mind that the smoothing scheme in Figure 12.3 has been set up with daily data in mind. When looking at data on an intraday basis, there is likelihood of running into intraday effects on the spread variance at market open and market close. One can expect that the spread variance is high around those periods and lower during the middle of

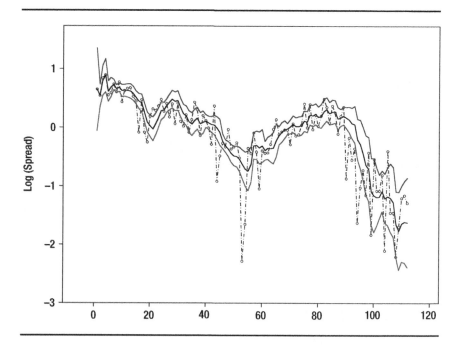

FIGURE 12.3   Kalman Smoothing with Confidence Bands (AZA-SEQU, lag 5).

the day. The constant arrival of information assumption is probably not correct under such circumstances.

SUMMARY

- The spread observed in the marketplace between two companies involved in a merger is likely to be distorted due to other market effects like the bid-ask spread effects and market maker inventory adjustments.
- The Kalman filtering approach is a suitable smoothing technique for estimating the actual spread levels.
- The filtered spread could be used for the risk-neutral probability and also assist in timing executions.

FURTHER READING MATERIAL

Kalman Filter

Harvey, A. C. *Time Series Models*, 2nd Edition. (Cambridge, Mass: MIT Press, 1993), pp. 82–104.

Model Choice

Kalaba, R., and T. Tesfatsion. "A Multicriteria Approach to Model Specification and Estimation." *Computational Statistics and Data Analysis* 21 (1996): 193–214.

Realized Volatility

Anderson, T. G., and others. "The Distribution of Exchange Rate Volatility." *Symposia 99, Statistical Issues in Risk Management*. Leonard N. Stern School of Business, April 1999.

APPENDIX

Kalman Filter Design: Lag 1

The state equation of the Kalman filter is given as

$$\hat{X}_{t|t-1} = 2\hat{X}_{t-1|t-1} - \hat{X}_{t-2|t-2}$$
$$\text{var}\left(\hat{X}_{t|t-1}\right) = 4\,\text{var}\left(\hat{X}_{t-1|t-1}\right) + \text{var}\left(\hat{X}_{t-2|t-2}\right) - 4\,\text{cov}\left(\hat{X}_{t-1|t-1}, \hat{X}_{t-2|t-2}\right)$$

The observation equation is given as

$$Y_t = X_t + \eta_t$$

The variance of Y_t is calculated as described in the discussion on the observation equation. We now define

$$g_t = \frac{\text{var}\left(Y_t\right)}{\text{var}\left(Y_t\right) + \text{var}\left(\hat{X}_{t|t-1}\right)}$$

where $g_t = 1 - K_t$, K_t is the Kalman gain as described in the standard predictor-corrector framework. The posteriori estimate of the state, and its variance is given as

$$\hat{X}_{t|t} = g_t \hat{X}_{t|t-1} + \left(1 - g_t\right)Y_t$$
$$\text{var}\left(\hat{X}_{t|t}\right) = \frac{\text{var}\left(\hat{X}_{t|t-1}\right)\text{var}\left(Y_t\right)}{\text{var}\left(\hat{X}_{t|t-1}\right) + \text{var}\left(Y_t\right)}$$

We note that the a posterori estimate is actually a convex combination of the a priori estimate and the observation. The value of g_t as computed here ensures that the variance of the resulting combination is a minimum. We now proceed to obtain a recursive relation for $\text{cov}\left(\hat{X}_{t-1}\hat{X}_{t-2}\right)$. The Kalman equation for the subscript $t - 1$ is

$$\hat{X}_{t-1|t-1} = g_{t-1}\hat{X}_{t-1|t-2} + \left(1 - g_{t-1}\right)Y_{t-1}$$

Substituting for $\hat{X}_{t-1|t-2}$, we have

$$\hat{X}_{t-1|t-1} = g_{t-1}\left(2\hat{X}_{t-2|t-2} - \hat{X}_{t-3|t-3}\right) + \left(1 - g_{t-1}\right)Y_{t-1}$$

Multiplying the above by $\hat{X}_{t-2}$ and evaluating the expected value, we have

$$\text{cov}\left(\hat{X}_{t-1|t-1}, \hat{X}_{t-2|t-2}\right) = g_{t-1}\left[2\,\text{var}\left(\hat{X}_{t-2|t-2}\right) - \text{cov}\left(\hat{X}_{t-2|t-2}, \hat{X}_{t-3|t-3}\right)\right]$$

Kalman Filter Design: Lag 2

In order to enhance readability, we use $\hat{X}_t$ and $\hat{X}_{t|t}$ interchangeably to denote the posteriori state estimate. The state equation of the Kalman filter is obtained as a first order approximation of the Taylor expansion about the current point. To do that, an estimate of the derivative is required. The previous design used the first difference of the previous step as an estimate of the derivative. In this design, the derivative is estimated with two sample points. The mean and variance of the first sample are as follows:

$$E(\text{sample1}) = \hat{X}_{t-1} - \hat{X}_{t-2}$$
$$\text{var}(\text{sample1}) = \text{var}\left(\hat{X}_{t-1}\right) + \text{var}\left(\hat{X}_{t-2}\right) - 2\,\text{cov}\left(\hat{X}_{t-1}, \hat{X}_{t-2}\right)$$

The mean and variance of the second sample are as follows:

$$E(\text{sample 2}) = \hat{X}_{t-2} + \hat{X}_{t-3}$$
$$\text{var}(\text{sample 2}) = \text{var}\left(\hat{X}_{t-2}\right) + \text{var}\left(\hat{X}_{t-3}\right) - 2\,\text{cov}\left(\hat{X}_{t-2}, \hat{X}_{t-3}\right)$$

The covariance between the two samples are as follows:

$$\text{cov}(\text{samples}) = \text{cov}\left[\left(\hat{X}_{t-1} - \hat{X}_{t-2}\right),\left(\hat{X}_{t-2} - \hat{X}_{t-3}\right)\right]$$
$$\text{cov}(\text{samples}) = \text{cov}\left(\hat{X}_{t-1}, \hat{X}_{t-2}\right) - \text{var}\left(\hat{X}_{t-2}\right) - \text{cov}\left(\hat{X}_{t-1}, \hat{X}_{t-3}\right) +$$
$$+ \text{cov}\left(\hat{X}_{t-2}, \hat{X}_{t-3}\right)$$

The minimum variance linear combination of the two samples is given by

$$r_t(\hat{X}_{t-1} - \hat{X}_{t-2}) + (1 - r_t)(\hat{X}_{t-2} - \hat{X}_{t-3})$$

where r_t is given as

$$r_t = \frac{\text{var}(\text{sample 2}) - \text{cov}(\text{samples})}{\text{var}(\text{sample 1}) + \text{var}(\text{sample 2}) - 2\,\text{cov}(\text{samples})}$$

Now the state equation is given as

$$\hat{X}_{t|t-1} = \hat{X}_{t-1} + r_t\left(\hat{X}_{t-1} - \hat{X}_{t-2}\right) + \left(1 - r_t\right)\left(\hat{X}_{t-2} - \hat{X}_{t-3}\right)$$

$$\hat{X}_{t|t-1} = \left(1 + r_t\right)\hat{X}_{t-1} + \left(1 - 2r_t\right)\hat{X}_{t-2} - \left(1 - r_t\right)\hat{X}_{t-3}$$

$$\text{var}\left(\hat{X}_{t|t-1}\right) = \left(1 + r_t\right)^2 \text{var}\left(\hat{X}_{t-1}\right) + \left(1 - 2r_t\right)^2 \text{var}\left(\hat{X}_{t-2}\right) + \left(1 - r_t\right)^2 \text{var}\left(\hat{X}_{t-3}\right)$$

$$+ 2\left(1 + r_t\right)\left(1 - 2r_t\right)\text{cov}\left(\hat{X}_{t-1}, \hat{X}_{t-2}\right)$$

$$- 2\left(1 + r_t\right)\left(1 - r_t\right)\text{cov}\left(\hat{X}_{t-1}, \hat{X}_{t-3}\right)$$

$$- 2\left(1 - 2r_t\right)\left(1 - r_t\right)\text{cov}\left(\hat{X}_{t-1}, \hat{X}_{t-3}\right)$$

The observation equation is given as

$$Y_t = \hat{X}_t + \eta_t$$

The variance of Y_t is calculated as described in the discussion of the observation equation. We now define

$$g_t = \frac{\text{var}\left(Y_t\right)}{\text{var}\left(Y_t\right) + \text{var}\left(\hat{X}_{t|t-1}\right)}$$

$g_t = 1 - K_t$, where K_t is the Kalman gain as described in the standard predictor-corrector framework. The Kalman equations providing the minimum variance linear estimate are as follows:

$$\hat{X}_{t|t} = g_t\hat{X}_{t|t-1} + \left(1 - g_t\right)Y_t$$

$$\text{var}\left(\hat{X}_{t|t}\right) = \frac{\text{var}\left(\hat{X}_{t|t-1}\right)\text{var}\left(Y_t\right)}{\text{var}\left(\hat{X}_{t|t-1}\right) + \text{var}\left(Y_t\right)}$$

We now proceed to obtain the recursive relation for $\text{cov}\left(\hat{X}_{t-1}, \hat{X}_{t-2}\right)$. The Kalman equation for subscript $t - 1$ is as follows:

$$X_{t|t-1} = g_{t-1}\hat{X}_{t-1|t-2} + \left(1 - g_t\right)Y_{t-1}$$

Substituting for $\hat{X}_{t-1|t-2}$, we have

$$\hat{X}_{t-1|t-1} = g_{t-1}\left[\left(1 + r_{t-1}\right)\hat{X}_{t-2} + \left(1 - 2r_{t-1}\right)\hat{X}_{t-3} -\right.$$
$$\left. - \left(1 - r_{t-1}\right)\hat{X}_{t-4}\right] + \left(1 - g_{t-1}\right)Y_{t-1}$$

Multiplying the above by $\hat{X}_{t-2}$ and evaluating the expected value, we have

$$\text{cov}\left(\hat{X}_{t-1}, \hat{X}_{t-2}\right) = g_{t-1}\left[\left(1 + r_{t-1}\right)\text{var}\left(\hat{X}_{t-2}\right) + \left(1 - 2r_{t-1}\right)\text{cov}\left(\hat{X}_{t-2}, \hat{X}_{t-3}\right) -\right.$$
$$\left. - \left(1 - r_{t-1}\right)\text{cov}\left(\hat{X}_{t-2}, \hat{X}_{t-4}\right)\right]$$

Multiplying by $\hat{X}_{t-3}$ and evaluating the expected value, we have

$$\text{cov}\left(\hat{X}_{t-1}, \hat{X}_{t-3}\right) = g_{t-1}\left[\left(1 + r_{t-1}\right)\text{cov}\left(\hat{X}_{t-2}, \hat{X}_{t-3}\right) + \left(1 - 2r_{t-1}\right)\text{var}\left(\hat{X}_{t-3}\right) -\right.$$
$$\left. - \left(1 - r_{t-1}\right)\text{cov}\left(\hat{X}_{t-3}, \hat{X}_{t-4}\right)\right]$$

Kalman Filter Design: Lag d (d >= 3)

To enhance readability, we use $\hat{X}_{t|t}$ and $\hat{X}_t$ interchangeably to denote the posteriori state estimate. The slope is estimated as the mean of the last d slope samples. This is given as

$$\frac{\hat{X}_{t-1} - \hat{X}_{t-1-d}}{d}$$

The state equation is therefore

$$\hat{X}_{t|t-1} = \hat{X}_{t-1} + \frac{\left(\hat{X}_{t-1} - \hat{X}_{t-1-d}\right)}{d}$$
$$\hat{X}_{t|t-1} = \left(1 + \frac{1}{d}\right)\hat{X}_{t-1} - \frac{1}{d}\hat{X}_{t-1-d}$$

The state variance is given by

$$\left(1 + \frac{1}{d}\right)^2 \text{var}\left(\hat{X}_{t-1}\right) + \frac{1}{d^2}\text{var}\left(\hat{X}_{t-1-d}\right)$$

the assumption being that $\hat{X}_{t-1}$ and $\hat{X}_{t-1-d}$ are not correlated. The observation equation is given as

$$Y_t = \hat{X}_t + \eta_t$$

The variance of Y_t is calculated as described in the discussion of the observation equation. We now define

$$g_t = \frac{\text{var}(Y_t)}{\text{var}(Y_t) + \text{var}(\hat{X}_{t|t-1})}$$

The Kalman equations providing the minimum variance linear estimate are as follows:

$$\hat{X}_{t|t} = g_t \hat{X}_{t|t-1} + (1 - g_t)Y_t$$

$$\text{var}(\hat{X}_{t|t}) = \frac{\text{var}(\hat{X}_{t|t-1})\,\text{var}(Y_t)}{\text{var}(\hat{X}_{t|t-1}) + \text{var}(Y_t)}$$

Index

Printed and bound by CPI Group (UK) Ltd, Croydon, CR0 4YY

23/04/2025

14660924-0001